© Assimil 2015
ISBN 978-2-7005-0644-0
ISSN 2266-1158

Graphic design: Atwazart

Italian

Jean-Pierre Guglielmi

Adapted for English speakers by Erin Brady

B.P. 25
94431 Chennevières sur Marne Cedex
France

This phrasebook doesn't claim to be a substitute for a language course, but if you devote a bit of time to reading it and learning a few useful phrases, you'll quickly find that you're able to participate in basic exchanges with Italian speakers, enriching your travel experience.

A word of advice: don't aim for perfection! Those you're speaking to will forgive any mistakes and appreciate your efforts to communicate in their language. The main thing is to leave your inhibitions behind and speak!

Section I — INTRODUCTION — 9

How to use this book 9
Italy: facts & figures 10
A bit of history 11
The Italian language 13

Section II — GETTING STARTED — 15

Day 1 to 21 15

Section III — CONVERSING — 57

First contact 57
  Greetings 57
  Offering wishes 58
  Agreeing and disagreeing 59
  Asking questions 59
  Making requests, thanking and excusing 59
  Making yourself understood 60

Meeting people 61
  Running into someone 61
  Introducing yourself or someone else 62
  Saying where you're from 62
  Giving your age 63
  Talking about your family 64
  Saying what you do 65
  Religion 67
  The weather 68
  Expressing opinions and feelings 69
  Invitations 70

Meeting up ...	71
... and chatting up	72
Time and the calendar	**73**
Talking about time	73
Days, months and seasons	75
Festivals and holidays	77
Asking for assistance	**78**
Emergencies	78
On the road	79
Signs, notices and abbreviations	**79**
Signs and notices	79
Abbreviations	80
Travelling	**81**
Passport control and customs	81
Money	82
Flying	82
Going by bus or train	83
Going by boat	86
Going by taxi	87
Biking and motorcycling	88
Renting a car	88
Driving	88
Getting around town	**92**
Finding your way around	92
Taking public transport	92
Sites and places of interest	94
Posting a letter	95
Making a phone call	96
Going online	97
Administration and forms	98

Reporting a theft or loss ... 99
At the bank ... 99
Going to a performance ... 100
At the hairdresser's ... 101

Outdoor activities ... **102**
Recreation ... 102
At the pool or beach ... 104
Camping ... 105
Trees and plants ... 107
Animals ... 108

Accommodation ... **111**
Making a reservation ... 111
At the hotel ... 112
Breakfast and services ... 113
Resolving issues ... 115

Eating and drinking ... **116**
At the restaurant ... 116
Specialities and traditional dishes ... 120
Food vocabulary ... 126
Cooking methods and sauces ... 130
Cheeses ... 134
Drinks ... 136
Other beverages ... 136

Shopping ... **137**
Shops and services ... 138
Laundry and dry cleaning ... 140
Shopping for clothes ... 141
Smoking ... 143
Photos ... 143
Souvenirs ... 144

Business meetings — 144
- Making an appointment — 144
- In the workplace — 145
- Business vocabulary — 146
- Conferences and trade shows — 146

Health — 147
- If you need medical attention — 147
- Symptoms — 148
- Health problems — 149
- Pains and body parts — 150
- Women's health — 151
- Getting treatment — 152
- At the dentist's — 153
- At the optician's — 153
- At the pharmacy — 153

INDEX

Introduction

↗ How to use this book

Section 1: Getting started in Italian

Can you spare a half an hour a day? Do you have three weeks ahead of you before your trip? In that case, jump in with the mini-lessons specially designed to familiarize you with Italian in just 21 days. These mini-lessons are aimed at beginners with no prior knowledge of Italian and will give you the basics you need to understand and address people in all sorts of situations.
• Discover the day's lesson, using the phonetic transcriptions to help you read the Italian out loud. Repeat it as many times as you wish!
• Check the translation in everyday English, as well as the word-for-word translation, if there is one, which will help you get used to the structure of the language.
• Read the notes that follow the lesson – these explain key linguistic points so you can apply them in other contexts.
• Finally, do the short exercise to consolidate what you've learned.

The next day, move on to the following lesson! Taking the time to do a little Italian each day is the most effective way to learn and remember it.

Section 2: Conversing

This section gives you the tools you'll need for dealing with a variety of situations in which you might find yourself during your trip. It provides useful vocabulary and expressions that you can use in a range of contexts. The Italian is accompanied by a translation, as well as a phonetic transcription that will help you pronounce it. This ready-to-use 'survival kit' is all you need to be an independent traveller!

↗ Italy: facts & figures

Surface area	301,340 km²
Population	61 million
Capital	Rome (population 2.7 million)
Land boundaries	Austria, France, Holy See (Vatican City), San Marino, Slovenia, Switzerland
Sea boundaries	Adriatic Sea, Ionian Sea, Mediterranean Sea, Tyrrhenian Sea
Government	Parliamentary republic; Italy is made up of 15 regions and 5 autonomous regions (Sardinia, Sicily, Trentino-Alto Adige/Südtirol, Aosta Valley, Friuli-Venezia Giulia)
National holiday	2 June (commemorating the vote to abolish the monarchy and establish a republic in 1946)
Religion	Predominantly Roman Catholic

Italy is a long, boot-shaped peninsula that extends into the Mediterranean. The island of Sicily, just off its southern tip, is only about 150 km from Tunisia in North Africa. Much of the country is rugged and mountainous; the Alps make up its northern border, and the Apennine Mountains stretch down its centre, with plains along either side. In the south, there are a number of volcanoes – Etna on Sicily is the largest active volcano in Europe. The climate in the south is hot and dry, while the north is cooler and wetter. Rich in historical, cultural and natural attractions, Italy boasts 50 UNESCO World Heritage Sites – more than any other country – and is one of the world's top five tourist destinations.

↗ A bit of history

Ancient Roman period

The Italian peninsula has been inhabited since prehistoric times, and was settled by civilizations such as the Etruscans and the Ancient Greeks, but the Roman period is the apex of its ancient history. Rome was founded in 753 BCE, and by the 2nd century BCE, the republic had become the dominant Mediterranean power. It later became an empire, reaching its greatest extent in 117 CE, with territories stretching across Europe and into North Africa and the Middle East. Centuries later, waves of Barbarian invasions led to the last Western Roman emperor being deposed in 476 CE. Successive conquests from different invaders divided the peninsula into various duchies, provinces and city-states. In 756, the Papacy was given authority over much of central Italy.

A mosaic of merchant republics

In the 12th and 13th centuries, independent city-states became the dominant form of government on the peninsula. For example, the prosperous merchant republic of Venice became an important maritime power, controlling much of northeastern Italy. Its rival, the Republic of Genoa, controlled Corsica, Sardinia and trading posts in the Black Sea and North Africa. In the 14th century, territorial disputes led to frequent wars between the city-states, followed by a series of foreign invasions starting in the late 1400s.

Towards Italian unity

After a long period of foreign domination and conflict, a movement to unify the different Italian states (the *Risorgimento* or 'resurgence') spread across the peninsula in the early 1800s. In 1861, Italy became a nation-state under King Victor-Emmanuel II, but lacked several territories, including Venice and Rome. These cities were finally annexed in 1870, completing Italian unification.

Modern Italy

At the beginning of the 20th century, Italy was confronted with both internal conflict and the external tensions that eventually led to World War I (1914–18). Italy joined the Allies, but felt betrayed by the Treaty of Versailles. The years following the war were marked by social and economic crises. Strikes, riots, factory occupations and a weak government created extreme political instability. This context allowed the National Fascist Party of Benito Mussolini to bring down the government in 1922. Mussolini's Fascist dictatorship would rule Italy for the next 20 years.

In World War II (1939–45), Mussolini declared support for Nazi Germany. By 1943, Italy was losing on every front – its cities were being heavily bombed, and its forces had suffered serious defeats in Greece, Russia and Africa. In July, the Allies invaded Sicily and Mussolini was ousted, leading to a civil war between pro- and anti-fascist forces. Mussolini was captured and executed in 1945, and Italy returned to a republic in 1946.

In the post-war years, Italy enjoyed an economic boom, growing rapidly and becoming a founding member of the European Union. In the last decades, Italy has faced a number of challenges, with a high public debt, political scandals and corruption. Nonetheless, it is the world's ninth-largest economy, reputed for its stylish consumer goods, and has a high quality of life ranking.

↗ The Italian language

From vernacular Latin to Italian

Like other Romance languages, Italian developed from the colloquial Latin spoken by those living in the Roman Empire. The different regions and even cities of the Italian peninsula had specific dialects, and for centuries these were used for people's daily interactions, while Classical Latin was used mainly for academic and religious texts. In the 14th century, the Florentine dialect used by Tuscan poets such as Dante spread throughout the peninsula. This became the basis of the standardized language known as Italian today.

The alphabet

There are 21 letters in the Italian alphabet, plus five more that appear in words borrowed from other languages, making it identical to the English alphabet.

a *[ah]*, **b** *[bee]*, **c** *[chee]*, **d** *[dee]*, **e** *[ay]*, **f** *[ef-feh]*, **g** *[jee]*, **h** *[ak-ka]*, **i** *[ee]*, **l** *[el-leh]*, **m** *[em-meh]*, **n** *[en-neh]*, **o** *[o]*, **p** *[pee]*, **q** *[koo]*, **r** *[erreh]*, **s** *[esseh]*, **t** *[tee]*, **u** *[oo]*, **v** *[vee]*, **z** *[dseta]* and **j** *[ee loonga]*, **k** *[kap-pa]*, **w** *[dop-pya voo]*, **x** *[eeks]*, **y** *[eepseelon]*

Pronunciation

Many of the letters are pronounced in a similar way to English, however, certain letter combinations can be tricky. For the right pronunciation, read the phonetic transcriptions out loud, paying attention to which vowel to stress (in bold). This will help you pick up the lilting intonation of **la bella lingua** *the beautiful language*. See the next page and the cover flaps for some specific tips.

Here are a few of the main difficulties for English speakers:

- **The 'c'**: This is a hard *[k]* in **ca**, **co**, **cu**, **chi** and **che**: e.g. **cosa** *[koza]* thing, **chilo** *[keelo]* kilo. But it is a *[ch]* in **ce**, **ci**, **cia**, **cio** and **ciu**: e.g. **certo** *[chayrto]* certain, **ciao** *[chaao]* hi/bye.

- **The 'g'**: This is a hard *[g]* in **ga**, **go**, **gu**, **ghi** and **ghe**: e.g. **gatto** *[gat-to]* cat, **funghi** *[foonghee]* mushrooms. But it is a *[j]* in **ge**, **gi**, **gia**, **gio** and **giu**: e.g. **gelato** *[jelato]* ice cream, **giovane** *[jovaneh]* young.

- **gli** is pronounced *[ly]* as in *million* – the **g** is silent.

- **gn** is pronounced *[ny]* as in *canyon* – the **g** is silent.

- **The silent 'h'**: The letter 'h' before a vowel is always silent.

- **The rolled 'r'**: The 'r' is trilled by vibrating the tip of the tongue against the roof of the mouth.

- **The 'sc'**: This is a hard *[sk]* in **sca**, **sco** and **scu**: e.g. **scala** *[skala]* stairs. But it is *[sh]* in **sce** and **sci**: e.g. **scendere** *[shendereh]* to descend, go down.

- **Double consonants**: In Italian words double consonants are pronounced more forcefully – almost as separate sounds with a slight pause between them. For example, **cane** *[caneh]* dog, but **canne** *[can-neh]* canes. With the exception of **ss** (pronounced *[ss]*), **rr** (pronounced as a longer trill) and a soft **cc** (pronounced *[ch]* but with more emphasis), we mark this with a hyphen.

So now you're ready to get started! **Buona fortuna!** *Good luck!*

Getting started

↗ Day 1

Ciao!
Hi!

1 Paolo è italiano.
paolo eh eetalyano
Paolo is Italian.

2 Maria è italiana.
mareea eh eetalyana
Maria is Italian.

3 Paolo e Maria sono italiani.
paolo ay mareea sono eetalyanee
Paolo and Maria are Italian.

Notes
Ciao! is an informal way both to greet someone or say goodbye: *Hi! Hello! Bye! See you!*

Every Italian noun is either masculine or feminine (even nouns that don't refer to people). An adjective that qualifies the noun has to agree with its gender. So when referring to a male or female, the ending of the word may be a bit different. Frequently, singular masculine words end in **-o** and singular feminine words end in **-a**: **italiano** *Italian* (m.); **italiana** *Italian* (f.).

An adjective also has to agree with a noun in number, i.e. whether it is singular or plural. In Italian, plurals are not formed by adding **-s**! The masculine singular ending **-o** changes to **-i**, and the feminine singular ending **-a** changes to **-e**: **italiani** *Italian* (m. pl.); **italiane** *Italian* (f. pl.). As in line 3 of the dialogue, the masculine form is used if a plural refers to both genders: **Paolo e Maria sono italiani.** *Paolo and Maria are Italian.*

The verb *to be* is **essere**. The third-person singular is **è** *he/she/it is*. Don't confuse it with the conjunction **e** *and*, which has no written accent. The third-person plural is **sono** *they are*.

To form a question in Italian, just change the intonation of the sentence – you don't need to change the order of the words: **Sono italiani.** *They are Italian.* **Sono italiani?** *Are they Italian?*

Practice – Translate the following sentences:
1. Are Paolo and Anna Italian?
2. Maria and Anna are Italian.
3. È italiana?
4. Ciao, Paolo!

Answers:
1. **Paolo e Anna sono italiani?**
2. **Maria e Anna sono italiane.**
3. Is she Italian?
4. Hi Paolo! *or* See you, Paolo!

↗ Day 2

I ragazzi
The kids

1 **Paolo è un ragazzo italiano.**
paolo eh oon ragat-tso eetalyano
Paolo is a boy Italian
Paolo is a young Italian man.

2 **Lui è italiano.**
looee eh eetalyano
He is Italian.

3 **Maria è una ragazza italiana.**
mareea eh oona ragat-tsa eetalyana
Maria is a girl Italian
Maria is a young Italian woman.

4 **Lei è italiana.**
ley eh eetalyana
She is Italian.

5 **Anche Marc e Maria sono ragazzi. Marc non è italiano.**
ankeh mark ay mareea sono ragat-tsee mark non eh eetalyano
also Marc and Maria are kids *(m.)*. marc not is Italian
Marc and Maria are also young people. Marc is not Italian.

Notes
Because Italian verbs conjugate differently in each person, you can tell who the subject is by the verb ending. Most often the subject pronouns **io** *I*, **tu** *you*, **lui** *he*, **lei** *she*, etc. are not used with the verb. In lines 2 and 4 the pronouns are included for emphasis. If the subject is clear, you would just say **è italiano** *he is Italian* or **è italiana** *she is Italian*.

To make a sentence negative, just put **non** before the verb: **è** *he/she/it is* → **non è** *he/she/it isn't*. The word for 'no' is simply **no**.

The noun **ragazzo** can mean *boy, kid, young man, guy, bloke*, etc. Like all regular nouns ending in **-o**, it has a plural form ending in **-i**: **ragazzi** *boys, kids*. If an **-o** noun refers to a person, there are also feminine forms: **ragazz**a *girl* and **ragazz**e *girls*.

Where word order is quite different from English, we've included a word-for-word translation. One difference is that adjectives usually come after a noun in Italian: **ragazze italiane** *Italian girls*.

In the title, we see the definite article *the*. This little word is a bit complicated in Italian because it has different forms depending on the noun's gender, number and the letter it starts with. For now, just note that **i** is one of the masculine plural forms of *the*.

Practice – Translate the following sentences.
1. Are they Italian? *(f.)*
2. He and she are young people.
3. **Anche Paolo e Anna sono ragazzi italiani.**
4. **Non è italiano.**

Answers:
1. **Sono italiane?**
2. **Lui e lei sono ragazzi.**
3. Paolo and Anna are also young Italians.
4. He isn't Italian.

↗ Day 3

Dove sei?
Where are you?

1 Ciao Paolo, sono Maria.
ch*aa*o p*a*olo s*o*no mar*ee*a
hi Paolo I-am Maria.
Hi Paolo, it's Maria.

2 Ciao Maria, dove sei?
ch*aa*o mar*ee*a d*o*veh sey
hi Maria where you-are *(informal)*
Hi Maria, where are you?

3 Sono a Roma con Marc.
s*o*no a r*o*ma kon mark
I'm in Rome with Marc.

4 Chi è Marc?
kee eh mark
Who is Marc?

5 Marc è un amico. Hai tempo per un caffè?
mark eh oon am*ee*ko I t*e*mpo payr oon kaf-f*eh*
Marc is a friend *(m.)*. you-have *(informal)* time for a coffee
Marc is a friend. Do you have time for a coffee?

6 Sì, certo!
see ch*ay*rto
yes certain
Yes, of course!

Notes

Italian has different ways of saying *you*. To address one person informally, use **tu** (second-person singular). To address more than one person, use **voi** (second-person plural). As **tu** is often omitted, the second-person singular verb indicates informal address. We'll see how to address someone formally later.

All the subject pronouns are shown below along with the present tense conjugation for the irregular verb **avere** to have:

singular	plural
(io) ho I have	(noi) abbiamo we have
(tu) hai you have (informal)	(voi) avete you have
(lui/lei) ha he/she/it has	(loro) hanno they have

And here is the present tense conjugation for the irregular verb **essere** to be (note that **sono** can mean I am or they are).

singular	plural
(io) sono I am	(noi) siamo we are
(tu) sei you are (informal)	(voi) siete you are
(lui/lei) è he/she/it is	(loro) sono they are

Some useful question words: **Chi?** Who? **Dove?** Where? The latter is sometimes contracted with **è** he/she/it is to form the question **dov'è** where is: **Dov'è Maria?** Where is Maria?

To say It's me on the phone: **Sono io.** ('I-am I')

Practice—Translate the following sentences:
1. Are you *(informal sing.)* in Rome?
2. You *(informal sing.)* don't have time for a coffee.
3. **Paolo e Maria sono amici.**
4. **Sì, sono a Roma.**

Answers:
1. **Sei a Roma?**
2. **Non hai tempo per un caffè.**
3. Paolo and Maria are friends.
4. Yes, I'm in Rome. *or* Yes, they are in Rome.

↗ Day 4

Benvenuto!
Welcome!

1 Ciao ragazzi!
ch*a*ao ragat-tsee
Hi guys!

2 Ciao Paolo, questo è il mio amico.
ch*a*ao p*a*olo k**way**sto eh eel m**ee**o am**ee**ko
Hi Paolo, this is ('the') my friend.

3 Ciao, sono Marc.
ch*a*ao s*o*no mark
Hi, I'm Marc.

4 Piacere. Benvenuto a Roma!
pyach**ay**reh baynvayn**oo**to a r*o*ma
pleasure. welcome *(m. sing.)* to Rome
Nice to meet you. Welcome to Rome!

5 Grazie.
gr*a*tsyeh
Thank you.

6 Ma parli italiano, complimenti!
ma p*a*rlee eetaly*a*no kompleem**ay**ntee
but you-speak *(informal sing.)* Italian, compliments
You speak Italian – well done!

Notes

Benvenuto! *Welcome!* is an adjective, so this is the form used when welcoming one man. The other forms are **Benvenuta!** (f. sing.), **Benvenuti!** (m. pl.) and **Benvenute!** (f. pl.).

Why is there a 'the' before 'my' in **il mio amico?** Apart from a few exceptions (e.g. when talking about a family member in the singular: **mio padre** *my father*), possessive adjectives (*my, your, his, her, its, our, their*) are always preceded by 'the'. Both words have to agree with the gender and number of what is possessed: **il mio ragazzo** *my boyfriend*, but **la mia ragazza** *my girlfriend*.

Another word that must agree with the gender and number of the noun it refers to is *this*: **questo** (m. sing.), **questa** (f. sing), **questi** (m. pl.) and **queste** (f. pl.). All this agreement may seem like a bit of a headache, but you'll soon get used to it. You can see the importance of remembering a noun's gender when you learn it!

In Italian, the present tense can be used to describe a general fact or an action going on at that very moment. So **parli italiano** can mean *you speak Italian* or *you are speaking Italian*.

Practice — Translate the following sentences:
1. The young man is Italian.
2. These young men aren't Italian.
3. **Con chi parli?**
4. **Questa è la mia amica.**

Answers:
1. Il ragazzo è italiano.
2. Questi ragazzi non sono italiani.
3. Who are you talking to?
4. This is my friend *(f.)*.

↗ Day 5

Al bar
At the bar

1. **Dove sono gli amici? Gli amici sono al bar in piazza.**
   doveh sono lyee ameechee lyee ameechee sono al bar een pyat-tsa
   where are the friends? the friends are at-the bar in square
   Where are the friends? The friends are at the bar in the square.

2. **Maria e Marc parlano del lavoro.**
   mareea ay mark parlano del lavoro
   Maria and Marc speak of-the work
   Maria and Marc talk about work.

3. **Paolo è ancora studente. Studia medicina a Roma.**
   paolo eh ankora stoodenteh stoodya maydeecheena a roma
   Paolo is still student. he-studies medicine at Rome
   Paolo is still a student. He studies medicine in Rome.

4. **Paolo parla degli studi.**
   paolo parla delyee stoodee
   Paolo speaks of-the studies
   Paolo talks about his studies.

Notes

A preposition + article often contract: **a + il → al** *to the*, **di + il → del** *of the* (sing.), **di + gli → degli** *of the* (pl.). As in lines 2 and 4, **del** and **degli** can be used in the sense of *about*.

Let's look at the forms of 'the'. The form depends on the gender and number of the noun, as well as the letters it starts with.

	singular	plural
before a consonant	il **ragazzo** (m.) *the boy* la **pizza** (f.) *the pizza*	i **ragazzi** *the boys* le **pizze** *the pizzas*
before s + consonant, z, gn, x, ps	lo **studente** (m.) *the student* la **spremuta** (f.) *juice*	gli **studenti** *the students* le **spremute** *juices*
before a vowel	l'**amico** (m.) *the friend* l'**amica** (f.) *the friend*	gli **amici** *the friends* le **amiche** *the friends*

Here is the present tense of regular verbs ending in **-are**:

parl**are** *to speak*	
(io) parl**o** *I speak*	(noi) parl**iamo** *we speak*
(tu) parl**i** *you speak* (informal)	(voi) parl**ate** *you speak*
(lui/lei) parl**a** *he/she speaks*	(loro) parl**ano*** *they speak*

* Note that the stress is on the first vowel: e.g. *[parlano]*.

Practice—Translate the following sentences:
1. Where do the students *(m. & f.)* study medicine?
2. Paolo is not at the bar in the square.
3. **Gli amici sono ancora al lavoro.**
4. **Parliamo degli amici.**

Answers:
1. **Dove studiano medicina gli studenti?**
2. **Paolo non è al bar in piazza.**
3. The friends are still at work.
4. We're talking about the friends.

↗ Day 6

Lo studente
The student (m.)

1 Come vanno gli studi?

komeh van-no lyee stoodee

how they-go the studies

How are your studies going?

2 Bene, ma non ho molto tempo libero.

beneh ma non o molto tempo leebayro

well but not I-have much time free

Fine, but I don't have much free time.

3 Vado ogni tanto al cinema. Ci vado con la mia amica.

vado onyee tanto al cheenema chee vado kon la meea ameeka

I-go every so-much to-the cinema. there I-go with the my friend (f.)

I go to the cinema with my girlfriend every once in a while.

4 Come sta Claudia?

komeh sta klaodya

How is Claudia?

5 Bene grazie. Fra poco ci raggiunge.

beneh gratsyeh fra poko chee raj-joonjeh

well thanks. within little us she-joins.

Fine, thank you. She'll join us soon.

Notes

Nouns ending in **-e** form the plural with **-i**, whether masculine or feminine: **il fiore** *flower* (m.) → **i fiori**; **la canzone** *song* (f.) → **le canzoni**. But if an **-e** noun refers to a person, some have different feminine forms: e.g. **lo studente** (m.); **la studentessa** (f.).

GETTING STARTED

Here is the present tense of regular verbs ending in **-ere**:

raggiung**ere** to join	
(io) raggiung**o** I join	(noi) raggiung**iamo** we join
(tu) raggiung**i** you join (inf.)	(voi) raggiung**ete** you join
(lui/lei) raggiung**e** he/she joins	(loro) raggiung**ono** they join

Note these two irregular verbs: **stare** to be, used for temporary states/locations (as opposed to **essere** to be, for unchanging conditions) and **andare** to go (**vado** I go, **vai** you go, **va** he/she/it goes, **andiamo** we go, **andate** you (pl.) go, **vanno** they go).

Direct object pronouns receive the action of a verb, as in line 5: **ci raggiunge** she joins us. They typically come before the verb in Italian. They are: **mi** me, **ti** you (inf.), **lo** him/it, **la** her/it, **ci** us (also an adverb meaning there), **vi** you (pl.), **li/le** them (m./f.).

Practice – Translate the following sentences:
1. How is Maria?
2. I'm going to the cinema with my boyfriend.
3. **Come vanno i ragazzi? Fra poco ci raggiungono?**
4. **Non ho molto tempo per gli studi.**

Answers:
1. Come sta Maria?
2. Vado al cinema con il mio amico.
3. How are the boys doing? Are they joining us soon?
4. I don't have much time for my studies.

↗ Day 7

Mi piace il jazz
I like jazz

1 **Gia e Sal vivono a Torino. Lei è giornalista, lui è pianista.**
   jeea ay sal veevono a toreeno ley eh jornaleesta looee eh pyaneesta
   Gia and Sal live in Turin. She is a journalist, he is a pianist.

2 **Quando escono, vanno spesso al bar con degli amici.**
   kwando eskono van-no spesso al bar kon delyee ameechee
   when they-leave they-go often to-the bar with some friends
   When they go out, they often go to a bar with friends.

3 **Sal suona il pianoforte jazz nel bar 'Arsenale'.**
   sal swona eel pyanoforteh jazz nel bar arsaynaleh
   Sal plays jazz piano in the bar the 'Arsenal'.

4 **A Gia piace molto il jazz.**
   a jeea pyacheh molto eel jazz
   to Gia it-appeals a-lot the jazz
   Gia likes jazz a lot.

Notes

Some new verbs: **vivere** *to live*, **suonare** *to play an instrument*, and the highly irregular **uscire** *to go out* → **io esco, tu esci, lui/lei esce, noi usciamo, voi uscite, loro escono**.

The verb for 'to like' is **piacere** *to please*, which conjugates like 'to appeal to'—so the verb agrees with what is pleasing: **Mi piace la musica.** ('To-me appeals the music'), but **Mi piacciono gli studi.** ('To-me appeal the studies').

GETTING STARTED

The **mi** in **mi piace** is an indirect object pronoun – these indicate to or for whom something occurs. Most are the same as the direct object pronouns, except for **gli** *to him/it*, **le** *to her/it* and **loro** *to them*. Or you can use the preposition **a** *to* followed by a strong object pronoun: **a me** *to me*, **a te** *to you*, **a lui** *to him/it*, **a lei** *to her/it*, **a noi** *to us*, **a voi** *to you*, **a loro** *to them*. **A me piace il libro** or **Mi piace il libro.** *I like the book.*

Here's a new contraction: **in + il → nel** *in the*. To express *some*, a contraction of **di** + plural definite article is used: **degli amici**.

Practice – Translate the following sentences:
1. I also live in Naples.
2. Do you *(informal sing.)* like Turin? Yes, of course, I like it!
3. **Dove andate? Andiamo a Torino.**
4. **Ci piace quando suona il pianoforte.**

Answers:
1. **Vivo anche a Napoli.**
2. **Ti piace Torino? Sì certo, mi piace!**
3. Where are you *(informal pl.)* going? We're going to Turin.
4. We like it when he/she plays the piano.

↗ Day 8

Vado spesso al caffè
I often go to the café

1 Quando sei in Inghilterra, vai spesso al caffè?
kw**a**ndo sey een eengheelt**ay**rra vI sp**ay**sso al kaf-f**e**h
When you're in England, do you often go to the café?

2 Capita ma non così spesso, in Italia però sì.
kap**ee**ta ma non koz**ee** sp**ay**sso een eet**a**lya payr**o** see
it-happens but not so often, in Italy however yes
Sometimes, though not a lot. But I often go in Italy.

3 Che prendi per colazione?
kay pr**e**ndee payr kolats**yo**neh
what you-take *(informal)* for breakfast
What do you have for breakfast?

4 Di solito, un caffè e una spremuta. I succhi sono favolosi!
dee s**o**leeto oon kaf-f**e**h ay **oo**na spraym**oo**ta ee s**oo**kee s**o**no
favol**o**zee
of usual a coffee and a fresh-squeezed-juice. the juices are fabulous
Usually, a coffee and a fresh juice. The juices are fantastic!

Notes

Like *the*, the indefinite article *a/an* has different forms:

	masc.	fem.
before a consonant	**un** ragazzo *a boy*	**una** ragazza *a girl*
before s + consonant, z, gn, x, ps	**uno** studente *a student*	**una** studentessa *a student*
before a vowel	**un** amico *a friend*	**un'**amica *a friend*

As we've seen, the indefinite article *some* is **di** + plural definite article, e.g. **dei ragazzi** *some boys*, **delle ragazze** *some girls*.

Another point about articles that you might have noticed in the last lesson is that no article is used to give a profession: **Lei/lui è giornalista.** ('She/He is journalist.')

In the plural, **il succo** *[eel sooko] juice* becomes **i succhi** *[ee sookee] juices*. Nouns ending in **-co**, **-go**, **-ca** and **-ga** add an **h** before the plural **-e** or **-i** ending to retain the hard *[k]* or *[g]* sound. But there are some exceptions, e.g. **amico** *[ameeko]* → **amici** *[ameechee]*. The feminine form follows the rule: **amica** *[ameeka]* → **amiche** *[ameekeh]*.

Practice – Translate the following sentences:
1. I'll have a fresh-squeezed juice.
2. Where are you *(informal sing.)* going?
3. **Usciamo al caffè per colazione.**
4. **L'amica di Francesco va spesso al cinema.**

Answers:
1. **Prendo una spremuta.**
2. **Dove vai?**
3. We're going out to a café for breakfast.
4. Francesco's girlfriend often goes to the cinema.

↗ Day 9

Dove sei?
Where are you?

1 **Luca prende il telefonino e chiama Gianna.**
looka prendeh eel taylayfoneeno ay kyama jan-na.
Luca takes his ('the') mobile phone and calls Gianna.

2 **Pronto? Dove sei?**
pronto doveh sey
Hello ('Ready')? Where are you?

3 **Sto uscendo dal metrò.**
sto ooshendo dal metro
I'm leaving ('from') the metro.

4 **Ordiniamo da bere. Vuoi bere qualcosa?**
ordeenyamo da bayreh vwoy bayreh kwalkoza
we-order to drink. you-want to-drink something
We're ordering drinks. Do you want something?

5 **Un analcolico, prego.**
oon analkoleeko prego
A nonalcoholic drink, please.

Notes

More verbs: **chiamare** *to call*, **ordinare** *to order*, **prendere** *to take* (or *to have* in the context of eating or drinking), **bere** *to drink* and **volere** *to want*. This useful verb is irregular: **voglio** *I want*, **vuoi** *you* (inf.) *want*, **vuole** *he/she wants*, **vogliamo** *we want*, **volete** *you* (pl.) *want*, **vogliono** *they want*.

To talk about an action in progress, a conjugated form of **stare** (or sometimes **andare**) + gerund (the *-ing* form) is used. This generally corresponds to *to be* + *-ing*: **sto uscendo** *I'm leaving (at this very moment)*. However, we've seen that the simple present is sometimes used to convey this meaning as well.

The gerund is formed by replacing an **-are** infinitive ending with **-ando**, or an **-ere** or **-ire** ending with **-endo**: **Sto aspettando.** *I am waiting.* (from **aspettare** *to wait*); **Sta venendo.** *She is coming.* (from **venire** *to come*).

To describe an imminent action, the construction is **stare per** + infinitive: **sto per partire** *I'm about to leave*.

Remember **prego**, which means *please, you're welcome, after you* and even *Pardon?* (literally, 'I beg' from **pregare** *to beg*).

Practice—Translate the following sentences:
1. I'm about to order [something] to drink.
2. Mario is [just] leaving the bar.
3. Mi chiama ogni tanto per parlare.
4. Ma non vi piacciono i succhi.

Answers:
1. Sto per ordinare da bere.
2. Mario sta uscendo dal bar.
3. Every so often he/she calls me to talk.
4. But you *(pl.)* don't like juice.

↗ Day 10

Lucia siede al tavolo
Lucia sits at the table

1   Enzo le chiede:
   endso lay kyaydeh
   Enzo to-her asks
   Enzo asks her:

2   Che cosa hai fatto stamattina?
   kay koza I fat-to stamat-teena
   what thing you-have done this-morning
   What did you do this morning?

3   Tante cose. Comunque sono passata dalla biblioteca a portare indietro i tuoi libri.
   tanteh kozeh komoonkweh sono passata dal-la beeblyoteka a portareh eendyaytro ee twoy leebree
   many things. however I-am passed (f.) from-the library to bring back the your books
   Many things. Even so, I went by the library to return your books.

4   Ah, li hai portati, grazie! Sei un tesoro, davvero!
   a lee I portatee gratsyeh sey oon tayzoro dav-vayro
   ah them you-have brought thanks! you-are a treasure really
   Ah, you returned them, thank you! You're a real angel!

Notes
Possessive adjectives (and articles) must agree with what is possessed: **i tuoi libri** *your books*. You'll find the complete list on the next page.

to give (**dare**); **chiede**vi *you were asking, used to ask* (**chiedere**); **veni**va *he/she was coming, used to come* (**venire**).

Line 5 has an example of the future tense: **partiremo** *we will leave*. But often the present tense can be used to talk about an action that will definitely happen: **Partiamo giovedì.** *We [will] leave Thursday.* **Rimaniamo tre giorni.** *We['ll] stay three days.*

To form the comparative (the equivalent of *-er*), Italian uses **più** *more* or **meno** *less* with the adjective: **più caro** *more expensive*, **meno caro** *less expensive, cheaper*. In line 3, **più a lungo** is the adverb *longer*.

Practice—Translate the following sentences:
1. I often used to go to the library.
2. We will leave on the train at 10:00 this morning.
3. **Rimanevano a Milano così poco.**
4. **Ha dato un concerto giovedì a Torino.**

Answers:
1. **Andavo spesso in biblioteca.**
2. **Partiremo / Partiamo in treno alle dieci stamattina.**
3. They were staying in Milan for such a short time.
4. He/she gave a concert on Thursday in Turin.

↗ Day 12

Cameriere!
Waiter!

1 Io ho un po' di fame e devo ritornare presto...
eeo o oon po dee fameh ay dayvo reetornareh presto
I have a little of hunger and I-must return soon
I'm a bit hungry and I have to go back soon ...

2 Dammi il menù. Hai già scelto?
dam-mee eel maynoo I ja shaylto
Give me the menu. Have you already chosen?

3 Io, prendo un tramezzino al prosciutto e verdure.
eeo prendo oon tramayd-dseeno al proshoot-to ay vayrdooreh
I I-take a sandwich at-the ham and vegetables
I'm having a prosciutto and vegetable sandwich.

4 Noi, un'insalata di stagione oggi.
noy oon eensalata dee stajoneh oj-jee
we a salad of season today
We're having a seasonal salad today.

5 Io, non so... Ho avuto fame tutto il giorno!
eeo non so o avooto fameh toot-to eel jorno
I not I-know... I-have had hunger all the day
As for me, I don't know ... I've been hungry all day!

Notes
In Italian, you 'have hunger' rather than 'are hungry': **avere fame**. Likewise, *to be thirsty* is **avere sete** 'to have thirst'.

The verb **dovere** expresses *to have to*, *must*. It is conjugated and followed by an infinitive: **devo mangiare** *I have to eat*, **devi ritornare** *you have to go back*, **dobbiamo rimanere** *we must stay*.

Dammi! *Give me!* is an informal command (from **dare** *to give*). The object pronoun **mi** *me* is attached to the end of the verb.

The useful verb **sapere** *to know* is irregular in the present tense: **io so** *I know*, **tu sai** *you know*, **lui/lei sa** *he/she knows*, **noi sappiamo** *we know*, **voi sapete** *you* (plural) *know*, **loro sanno** *they know*.

The present perfect of **avere** (i.e. 'to have had') is formed with **avere** (in the present tense) + the past participle of **avere**.

ho avuto *I have had*	abbiamo avuto *we have had*
hai avuto *you have had*	avete avuto *you* (pl.) *have had*
ha avuto *he/she/it has had*	hanno avuto *they have had*

Practice—Translate the following sentences:
1. The young men have already chosen.
2. You *(informal sing.)* must go back to work soon.
3. **A loro non piacciono i tramezzini.**
4. **Abbiamo avuto il piacere di servirvi.**

Answers:
1. **I ragazzi hanno già scelto.**
2. **Devi ritornare presto al lavoro.**
3. They don't like sandwiches.
4. We have had the pleasure of serving you.

↗ Day 13

Ordinare
Ordering

1 Siete stati serviti? Avete deciso?
syayteh statee sayrveetee avayteh daycheezo
Have you (pl.) been served? Have you (pl.) decided?

2 Sì, allora due insalate di stagione e un panino.
see al-lora dooeh eensalateh dee stajoneh eh oon paneeno
Yes ... so, two seasonal salads and a filled roll.

3 Da bere?
da bayreh
[And] to drink?

4 Una bottiglia d'acqua minerale e due birre alla spina.
oona bot-teelya dakwa meenayraleh ay dooeh beerreh al-la speena
A bottle of mineral water and two draught beers ('to-the tap').

Notes

The present perfect of **essere** (i.e. 'to have been') is formed with **essere** (in the present tense) + the past participle of **stare**.

sono stato/-a *I have been* (m./f.)	siamo stati/-e *we have been*
sei stato/-a *you have been*	siete stati/-e *you have been*
è stato/-a *he/she/it has been*	sono stati/-e *they have been*

When the auxiliary verb is **essere**, the ending has to agree in gender and number with the subject: **sono stato chiamato** *I* (m.) *have been asked*, **sei stata chiamata** *you* (f.) *have been asked*, **siamo stati chiamati** *we* (m.) *have been asked*, etc.

Here is the present tense of regular verbs ending in **-ire**:

serv**ire** to serve	
(io) servo I serve	**(noi) serv**iamo we serve
(tu) servi you serve (informal)	**(voi) serv**ite you serve
(lui/lei) serve he/she serves	**(loro) serv**ono they serve

Many **-ire** verbs have a spelling change in which **-isc-** is inserted between the verb stem and the conjugation ending in certain persons: e.g. **preferire** to prefer → **preferisco** I prefer, **preferisci** you prefer, **preferisce** he/she prefers, **preferiscono** they prefer.

Another example is **finire** to finish → **io finisco, tu finisci, lui/lei finisce, noi finiamo, voi finite, loro finiscono**.

Practice—Translate the following sentences:
1. Where have you *(m. pl.)* been?
2. They [will] finish at 7:00 today.
3. Il concerto sta per finire.
4. Lei esce ogni mattina alle otto.

Answers:
1. **Dove siete stati?**
2. **Finiscono alle sette oggi.**
3. The concert is about to end.
4. She goes out every morning at 8:00.

↗ Day 14

Un caffè al caffè
A coffee at the café

1 **In questo caffè il cibo è incredibile e pure conveniente.**
   een kwaysto kaf-feh eel cheebo eh eenkraydeebeeleh ay pooreh konvaynyaynteh
   In this café the food is incredible and yet affordable.

2 **Volete un caffè?**
   volayteh oon kaf-feh
   Do you (pl.) want a coffee?

3 **Certo, vorrei un macchiato.**
   chayrto vorrey oon mak-kyato
   Sure, I would like an espresso with a dash of milk.

4 **E io, un ristretto.**
   ay eeo oon reestret-to
   And for me, a short shot of espresso.

5 **Cameriere! Un macchiato per lei, due ristretti per loro e un lungo per me, per favore.**
   kamayryayreh oon mak-kyato payr ley dooeh reestrayt-tee payr loro ay oon loongo payr may payr favoreh
   Waiter! A macchiato for her, two ristrettos for them, and an espresso with extra water for me, please.

Notes
In this lesson we have an example of the conditional. In English this is formed with 'would', but in Italian an ending is added to the verb: **partire** *to leave* → **partirei** *I would leave*, **partiresti**,

partirebbe, **partiremmo**, **partireste**, **partirebbero**. In **-are** verbs, the **-a** also changes to **-e**: **parlare** → **parlerei** *I would speak*.

The conditional is very useful for asking for something politely; especially with the irregular verb **volere** *to want* → **vorrei** *I would like* ('would want'), **vorrebbe** *he/she would like*, **vorremmo** *we would like*, etc.

As we've seen, when a preposition is used with a definite article, they often contract. Here are the main contracted forms:

		a *at*	in *in*	di *of*	da *from*	su *on*	con *with*
masc. sing.	il	al	nel	del	dal	sul	col
	lo	allo	nello	dello	dallo	sullo	–
	l'	all'	nell'	dell'	dall'	sull'	–
fem. sing.	la	alla	nella	della	dalla	sulla	–
	l'	all'	nell'	dell'	dall'	sull'	–
masc pl.	i	ai	nei	dei	dai	sui	coi
	gli	agli	negli	degli	dagli	sugli	–
fem. pl.	le	alle	nelle	delle	dalle	sulle	–

Practice – Translate the following sentences:
1. We would like two draught beers, please.
2. The bottles are on the table.
3. Devo uscire presto.
4. Il tempo degli studi non è così lungo.

Answers:
1. Vorremmo due birre alla spina, per favore.
2. Le bottiglie stanno sul tavolo.
3. I have to go out soon.
4. The course ('time of the studies') isn't so long.

↗ Day 15

Le spese
Shopping ('the purchases')

1 Devo fare delle spese.
   dayvo fareh del-leh spayzeh
   I have to do some shopping.

2 Io ti accompagnerò con piacere.
   eeo tee ak-kompanyayro kon pyachayreh
   I you will-accompany with pleasure
   I'll come with you gladly.

3 Che stai cercando?
   kay stI chayrkando
   What are you looking for ('searching')?

4 Vorrei un paio di scarpe.
   vorrey oon pIo dee skarpeh
   I would like a pair of shoes.

5 Bene, i saldi non sono ancora finiti, approfittiamone!
   beneh ee saldee non sono ankora feeneetee ap-profeet-tyamoneh
   fine the sales not are yet finished, we-profit-of-them
   Good, the sales are still on. Let's take advantage of them!

Notes
The future tense in English is formed with 'will', but in Italian an ending is added to the verb: **prendere** *to take* → **io prenderò** *I will take*, **tu prenderai**, **lui/lei prenderà**, **noi prenderemo**, **voi prenderete**, **loro prenderanno**. In **-are** verbs, the **-a** also changes to **-e**: **parlare** → **parlerò** *I will speak*.

La spesa ('the purchase') is used to mean *the shopping*, i.e. grocery shopping, whereas **le spese** ('the purchases') refers to shopping for pleasure.

The **noi** *we* command (which is the same as the first-person plural present) translates to 'Let's …': **Andiamo!** *Let's go!* **Mangiamo!** *Let's eat!* **Approfittiamo!** *Let's make the most of it!*

In line 5 we see the pronoun **ne** *of it, of them* attached to the end of the **noi** command: **approfittiamone** *let's take advantage of them*. Although object pronouns usually come before the verb, they are attached to the end of commands as well as the infinitive form (in this case, the final **-e** is omitted): **le chiedo** *I ask her*, **devo chiederle** *I have to ask her*.

Practice—Translate the following sentences:
1. I don't know what I'm looking for
2. You *(informal sing.)* will like these shoes.
3. **Devi approfittarne.**
4. **Vorrei chiedergli di venire con me.**

Answers:
1. **Non so che sto cercando.**
2. **Ti piaceranno queste scarpe.**
3. You *(informal sing.)* have to make the most of it.
4. I would like to ask him to come with me.

↗ Day 16

Scarpe a buon prezzo
Shoes at a good price

1 Stamattina ho visto un negozio vicino all'albergo...
stamat-teena o veesto oon naygotsyo veecheeno al-lalbayrgo
This morning I saw a store near the hotel,

2 ma era un po' caro però.
ma era oon po karo payro
but it was a little expensive ('however').

3 Tu conosci bene la città.
too konoshee beneh la cheet-ta
You know the city well.

4 Certo! In quella strada ci sono scarpe a buon prezzo.
chayrto een kwayl-la strada chee sono skarpeh a bwon pret-tso
Of course! In that street there are shoes at a good price.

5 Benissimo, andiamoci questo pomeriggio!
beneessemo andyamochee kwaysto pomayreej-jo
Great ('very well'), let's go there this afternoon!

Notes
Note the irregular imperfect form **era** *it was* (from **essere**).

We've seen **sapere** *to know (a fact)* – **conoscere** is *to know* as in *to be familiar with* or *to be acquainted with*.

In line 1, **visto** *seen* is the irregular past participle of **vedere** *to see*. Here are some others: **preso** *taken* (**prendere** *to take*); **detto** *said* (**dire** *to say*); **fatto** *done/made* (**fare** *to do/make*); **chiesto** *asked* (**chiedere** *to ask*); **scelto** *chosen* (**scegliere** *to choose*); **rimasto** *stayed* (**rimanere** *to stay*).

In line 4, **ci** is the adverb *here* or *there* (not to be confused with the pronoun **ci** *us*). It is used in the very useful phrase **c'è** (**ci + è**) *there is* and **ci sono** *there are*. In line 5, we see that the adverb **ci** can be attached to the end of a command: **Andiamoci!** *Let's go there!*

The adjective *that* follows the same spelling rules as the definite article (lesson 5): **quel, quello, quell', quella, quei, quegli, quelle**. E.g. **quel negozio** *that shop*; **quella città** *that city*, etc.

The ending **-issimo/-a/-i/-e** conveys intensity, as in 'very': **carissimo** *very expensive* (or *very dear, cherished*).

Practice—Translate the following sentences:
1. There is a very good shop in that street.
2. The food was incredible.
3. **Che cosa ha fatto?**
4. **Non so, non lo conosco.**

Answers:
1. **C'è un buonissimo negozio in quella strada.**
2. **Il cibo era incredibile.**
3. What did he/she do?
4. I don't know, I don't know him.

↗ Day 17

Nel negozio
In the store

1 Entri pure... Mi dica, signorina.
entree pooreh mee deeka seenyoreena
enter *(formal)* by-all-means ... me you-tell young lady
Please, come in! How can I help you, miss?

2 Vorrei provare quelle scarpe in vetrina, in marrone.
vorrey provareh kwayl-leh skarpeh een vaytreena een marroneh
I would like to try on those shoes in [the] window, in brown.

3 Che numero porta?
kay noomayro porta
what number you-wear *(formal)*
What's your size?

4 Il 38 (trentotto).
eel trayntot-to
38.

5 Un attimo, per piacere... Ecco il 38 in marrone.
oon at-teemo per pyachayreh ek-ko eel trayntot-to een marroneh
a moment for favour ... here-is the 38 in brown
One moment, please ... Here is size 38 in brown.

Notes

In a service situation like this, formal address is used in Italian. To ask someone a question in a polite way, you use the third-person singular: **Che numero porta?** *What size do you wear?* (informal: **Che numero porti?**); **Vuole provarlo?** *Do you want to try it on?* (informal: **Vuoi provarlo?**). The formal subject pronoun for *you* is **Lei** (formal pronouns are capitalized).

GETTING STARTED

This lesson also has some examples of the formal imperative: **Entri!** *Come in!* (informal: **Entra!**) **Dica!** *Tell!* (informal: **Di!**). More on this later.

Some common verbs are highly irregular in the present tense.

dire *to say*	bere *to drink*	fare *to do/make*
dico *I say*	**bevo**	**faccio**
dici *you say* (inf. sing.)	**bevi**	**fai**
dice *he/she says*	**beve**	**fa**
diciamo *we say*	**beviamo**	**facciamo**
dite *you say* (pl.)	**bevete**	**fate**
dicono *they say*	**bevono**	**fanno**

Certain other tenses also have the same irregularity in the stem, e.g. the imperfect: **dic**evo *I was saying* (or *I used to say*), **bev**evo *I was drinking/used to drink*, **fac**evo *I was doing/used to do*.

Practice—Translate the following sentences:
1. What are we doing this afternoon?
2. I would like to go shopping with a friend *(f.)*.
3. **Ci sono tanti negozi!**
4. **Che sta cercando?**

Answers:
1. **Che cosa facciamo questo pomeriggio?**
2. **Vorrei fare delle spese con un'amica.**
3. There are so many stores!
4. What is he/she looking for? / What are you *(formal)* looking for?

↗ Day 18

Al telefono
On the phone

1 Pronto?
pronto
Hello? ('Ready?')

2 Ciao Luigi, sono io. Ti piacerebbe andare al cinema domani?
chaao lweejee sono eeo tee pyachayreb-beh andareh al cheenayma domanee
Hi Luigi, it's me. Would you like to go to the cinema tomorrow?

3 Mi dispiace davvero, ma non ci posso andare.
mee deespyacheh dav-vayro ma non chee posso andareh
me it-displeases truly but not there can-I go
I'm really sorry, but I can't go.

4 Dai! Vengono anche Francesca e Sergio.
dI vayngono ankeh franchayska ay sayrjo
Come on ('Give')! Francesca and Sergio are coming too.

Notes

The way to say *I'm sorry* in Italian is **mi dispiace** ('it displeases me') or **scusa** (informal) / **scusi** (formal).

Let's look at the present tense conjugations of the irregular verbs **dovere** *to have to, 'must'* and **potere** *to be able to, 'can'.* These verbs are usually followed by an infinitive: **dobbiamo chiamare** *we have to call*; **posso andare** *I can go*.

dovere to have to	potere to be able to
devo or **debbo** I have to	**posso** I can
devi you have to (inf. sing.)	**puoi** you can (inf. sing.)
deve he/she/it has to or you have to (formal)	**può** he/she/it can or you can (formal)
dobbiamo we have to	**possiamo** we can
dovete you have to (pl.)	**potete** you can (pl.)
devono or **debbono** they have to	**possono** they can

To make **dovere** *to have to* more polite (i.e. *should* rather than *must*), use the conditional: **dovrei** *I should*, **dovresti** *you* (inf.) *should*, **dovrebbe** *he/she/you* (formal) *should*, **dovremmo** *we should*, **dovreste** *you* (pl.) *should*, **dovrebbero** *they should*.

Practice—Translate the following sentences:
1. You *(formal)* should come.
2. I'm sorry, I can't.
3. **Puoi andare al caffè domani? Gli piacerebbe davvero.**
4. **La ragazza vorrebbe provare quelle scarpe.**

Answers:
1. **Dovrebbe venire.**
2. **Mi dispiace, non posso.**
3. Can you go to the café tomorrow? He would really like that.
4. The young woman would like to try on those shoes.

↗ Day 19

Come ti chiami?
What's your name?

1 Rosa, conosci mio figlio?
roza konoshee meeo feelyo
Rosa, do you know my son?

2 No! Come ti chiami?
no komeh tee kyamee
no! how yourself you-call *(informal)*
No! What's your name?

3 Mi chiamo Lorenzo. Ho nove anni.
mee kyamo lorendso o noveh an-nee
myself I-call Lorenzo. I-have nine years
My name is Lorenzo. I'm nine years old.

4 Bene! Che cosa fai per divertirti?
beneh kay koza fI payr deevayrteertee
fine! what thing you-do for to-enjoy-yourself
OK! What do you do for fun?

Notes

Mi chiamo ('I call myself') is the equivalent of *My name is*. The verb **chiamarsi** *to be called* includes a reflexive pronoun that indicates that the subject is performing the action on itself (e.g. *myself, yourself, himself*, etc.). Here is the full conjugation of a reflexive verb (**divertirsi** *to enjoy oneself, to have fun*):

mi **diverto** *I enjoy myself*	ci **divertiamo** *we enjoy ourselves*
ti **diverti** *you enjoy yourself*	vi **divertite** *you enjoy yourselves*
si **diverte** *he/she/one enjoys himself/herself/oneself*	si **divertono** *they enjoy themselves*

GETTING STARTED

The pronoun is part of a reflexive verb, it can't be left out. Another important thing to know about reflexive verbs is that in the present perfect, they always conjugate with the auxiliary verb **essere** (rather than **avere**). This means that the past participle needs to agree in gender and number with the subject: **mi sono divertito** *I had fun* (m. sing.), **mi sono divertita** *I had fun* (f. sing.), **ci siamo divertiti** *we had fun* (m. pl.), **ci siamo divertite** *we had fun* (f. pl.).

Reflexive pronouns can also be used in the sense of *each other*: **ci vediamo ogni sera** *we see each other every evening*.

Practice — Translate the following sentences:
1. What are your names?
2. They speak to each other often.
3. **Potete venire domani sera?**
4. **Dovresti chiamare tuo figlio.**

Answers:
1. **Come vi chiamate?**
2. **Si parlano spesso.**
3. Can you *(pl.)* come tomorrow evening?
4. You *(informal sing.)* should call your son.

↗ Day 20

Che ne pensi?
What do you think of it?

1 Allora come era quel film ieri sera?
al-lora komeh era kwayl feelm yayree sayra
So how was that film yesterday evening?

2 Bello, bello. Era un thriller stupendo.
bel-lo bel-lo era oon treel-layr stoopendo
Very good. It was a fantastic thriller.

3 In effetti era abbastanza complesso. Alla fine…
een ef-fayt-tee era ab-bastantsa komplesso al-la feeneh
In fact, it was fairly complex. At the end …

4 Non dirlo ti prego! Se magari lo vedo anch'io…
non deerlo tee prego say magaree lo vaydo ankeeo
not say-it you I-beg! if maybe it I-see also-I
Don't say anything, please! I might go see it too …

Notes

Don't forget the pronoun **ne** *of/about it*: **Che ne sai?** *What do you know about it?* **Ne voglio ancora!** *I want some more of that!*

Since the imperfect is used for describing something in the past, it is useful to know the forms for **essere** *to be*: **ero** *I was*, **eri** *you (informal) were*, **era** *he/she/it was, you (formal) were*, **eravamo** *we were*, **eravate** *you (pl.) were*, **erano** *they were*.

A negative informal **tu** command is formed with **non** + infinitive: **Non dire!** *Don't tell!* (The final **-e** of the infinitive is dropped if a

GETTING STARTED

pronoun is attached at the end: **Non dirmi!** *Don't tell me!*) A negative **voi** command (to address more than one person) is simple: **non** + second-person plural: **Non parlate!** *Don't talk!* (pl.). We'll look at formal commands in the next lesson.

To make a request more polite, you can add **pregare di** ('to beg to'): **Ti prego di dirmi!** *Please tell me!* ('I beg you to tell me!') **La prego di farlo.** *Please do it.* ('I beg you [formal] to do it.') (the formal object pronoun for *you* is **La** – it is always capitalized).

Practice – Translate the following sentences:
1. It *(f.)* was rather complicated.
2. Yesterday evening I saw a film. Don't see it! *(informal sing.)*
3. **In effetti non mi hanno chiesto di venire stasera.**
4. **Magari conosci dei film italiani?**

Answers:
1. **Era abbastanza complessa.**
2. **Ieri sera, ho visto un film. Non vederlo!**
3. In fact, they didn't ask me to come this evening.
4. Perhaps you know some Italian films?

↗ Day 21

Alla stazione Roma Termini
At the Termini Station in Rome

1 **Da che binario parte il treno?**
   da kay beenaryo parteh eel trayno
   From what platform does the train leave?

2 **Dal binario quattro… Guardi, la seconda classe è laggiù.**
   dal beenaryo kwat-tro gwardee la saykonda klasseh eh laj-joo
   From platform 4 … Look, second class is over there.

3 **Controllo dei biglietti, prego!**
   kontrol-lo day beelyayt-tee prego
   Inspection of your ('the') tickets, please!

4 **Eccoli. Scusi, ci sarà un ritardo?**
   ek-kolee skoozee chee sara oon reetardo
   Here they are. Excuse me, will there be a delay?

5 **Non penso, ecco i vostri biglietti. Buon viaggio!**
   non penso ek-ko ee vostree beelyayt-tee bwon vyaj-jo
   I don't think [so]. Here [are] your tickets. [Have a] good trip!

Notes

When speaking to someone older who you don't know well, in a hotel, store or restaurant or in formal situations, use the third-person singular: **Può ripetere?** *Can you* (formal) *repeat that?*

Note the very useful (irregular) future tense of **essere**: **sarò** *I will be*, **sarai** *you* (inf. sing.) *will be*, **sarà** *he/she/it/you* (formal) *will be*, **saremo** *we will be*, **sarete** *you* (plural) *will be*, **saranno** *they will be*. And the useful expression: **ci sarà** *there will be*.

To make a command in the formal singular (for regular verbs), just change the final vowel of the **tu** imperative:
- **a → i** for **-are** verbs:

Guarda! (informal) → **Guardi!** (formal) *Look!*
Scusa! (informal) → **Scusi!** (formal) *Excuse me!*
Entra! (informal) → **Entri!** (formal) *Come in!*
- **i → a** for **-ere** and **-ire** verbs:

Prendi! (informal) → **Prenda!** (formal) *Take!*
Finisci! (informal) → **Finisca!** (formal) *Finish!*
Parti! (informal) → **Parta!** (formal) *Leave!*

And some common irregular forms:
Vai! (informal) → **Vada!** (formal) *Go!* (**andare**)
Vieni! (informal) → **Venga!** (formal) *Come!* (**venire**)
Dai! (informal) → **Dia!** (formal) *Give!* (**dare**)
Di! (informal) → **Dica!** (formal) *Tell!* (**dire**)
Fai! (informal) → **Faccia!** (formal) *Do!* (**fare**)

To make a formal command negative, just add **non**:
Non parli! *Don't talk!* **Non faccia!** *Don't do it!*

Practice—Translate the following sentences:
1. Go *(formal)* to the station.
2. Excuse me *(formal)*, where is platform 2?
3. **Mi dispiace davvero, ma ci sarà un ritardo.**
4. **La prego, entri pure.**

Answers:
1. **Vada alla stazione.**
2. **Scusi, dov'è il binario due?**
3. I am very sorry, but there will be a delay.
4. Please, do come in *(formal)*.

Conversing

↗ First contact

Italians often use the informal **tu** *you* (with the second-person singular verb) – especially the younger generation. But it's still useful to know the formal **Lei** *you* (used with the third-person singular verb), especially for service contexts. (All formal pronouns, **Lei**, **La**, **Le**, etc., are capitalized –though they appear to be feminine, they are used to address both genders.)

Greetings

Saying hello & taking leave

Hello! ('Good day!')	**Buon giorno!**	bwon jorno
Hi! / Bye!	**Ciao!**	chaao
Good evening!	**Buonasera!**	bwonas**ay**ra
Have a good evening!	**Buona serata!**	b**wo**na sayrata
Goodnight!	**Buona notte!**	b**wo**na not-teh
Goodbye!	**Arrivederci!**	arreevay**day**rchee
See you soon!	**A presto! / Ci vediamo!**	a pr**e**sto / chee vayd**ya**mo
Farewell!	**Addio!**	ad-d**ee**o

The most common way to say goodbye is **Ciao!** *[chaao]*.

Addressing someone

Mrs / madam	**la signora**	la seen**yo**ra
Miss / young lady	**la signorina**	la seenyor**ee**na
Mr / sir / gentleman	**il signor(e)**	eel seen**yo**reh

To excuse yourself, you say **Scusa!** [sk**oo**za] if speaking to one person informally, or:

Excuse me!
Scusi! *(formal sing.)* / **Scusate!** *(to more than one person)*
sk**oo**zee / skooz**a**teh

Or if you want to pass through a group of people:

Excuse me ...
Permesso...
payrm**ay**sso

Making yourself understood

Do you speak ...	Parla... *(formal)*	parla
English?	inglese?	eengl**ay**zeh
French?	francese?	franch**ay**zeh
German?	tedesco?	tayd**ay**sko
Italian?	italiano?	eetal**ya**no
Spanish?	spagnolo?	span**yo**lo

I don't understand.
Non capisco.
non kap**ee**sko

Could you repeat that, please?
Può ripetere, per favore? *(formal)*
pwo reep**e**tayreh payr fav**o**reh

What does that mean?
Che cosa significa?
kay k**o**za seeny**ee**feeka

↗ Meeting people

Running into someone

Among friends and acquaintances, Italians use **tu**, reserving **Lei** for speaking to older people, superiors or in formal contexts. It's common for friends and relatives to greet each other with **un bacio** *a kiss* on each cheek.

How's it going?	**Come va?**	*komeh va*
How are you?	**Come stai?** *(inf.)*	*komeh stI*
Everything okay?	**Tutto a posto?**	*toot-to aposto*
Fine, thank you.	**Bene, grazie.**	*beneh gratsyeh*
Very well.	**Molto bene.**	*molto beneh*
Very well, and you?	**Benissimo, e tu?** *(inf.)*	*bayneesseemo ay too*
And you?	**E Lei?** *(formal)*	*ay ley*
So so.	**Così così.**	*kozee kozee*
Not so well.	**Non così bene.**	*non kozee beneh*
Excuse me.	**Mi scusi.** *(formal)*	*mee skoozee*

In more formal settings, some options are:

Hello Mr Farina, how are you?
Buongiorno signor Farina, come sta?
bwonjorno seenyor fareena komeh sta

Fine, thank you – and you?
Bene, grazie, e Lei?
beneh gratsyeh ay ley

Very well, thank you. How is Mrs Carloni?
Molto bene, grazie. Come sta la signora Carloni?
molto beneh gratsyeh komeh sta la seenyora karlonee

CONVERSING

Introducing yourself or someone else

What's your name?
Come ti chiami? *(inf.)* / **Come si chiama?** *(formal)*
komeh tee kyamee / komeh see kyama

My name is ...
Mi chiamo...
mee kyamo

This is my friend Stefan / my friend Anita.
Le presento il mio amico Stefan / la mia amica Anita. *(formal)*
leh prayzento eel meeo ameeko ... / la meea ameeka ...

Delighted!
Molto lieto/-a! *(m./f.)*
molto lyayto/-a

Pleased to meet you!
Piacere!
pyachayreh

Saying where you're from

Where are you from?
Da dove viene? *(formal)* / **Da dove vieni?** *(inf.)*
da doveh vyayneh / da doveh vyaynee

If you want to avoid using an adjective and thus having to choose the appropriate masculine or feminine form, you can just answer by giving the name of the country you come from: **Vengo dal Regno Unito.** *[raynyo ooneeto] I come from the UK.*

I come ...	Vengo...	vengo
from England.	dall'Inghilterra.	dal-leengheelterra
from Ireland.	dall'Irlanda.	dal-leerlanda
from South Africa.	dal Sudafrica.	dal soodafreeka

We come ...	Veniamo...	vaynyamo
from the United States.	dagli Stati Uniti.	dalyee statee ooneetee
from Australia.	dall'Australia.	dal-laostralya
He/she comes from Canada.	Viene dal Canada.	vyayneh dal kanada
I also come from New Zealand.	Anch'io vengo dalla Nuova Zelanda.	ankeeo vengo dal-la nwova zaylanda

Where do you live?
Dove stai *(inf.)* **/ sta** *(formal)* **di casa?**
doveh stI / sta dee kaza

I live in London.
Sto a Londra.
sto a londra

What is your address?
Qual è il Suo *(formal)* **/ il tuo** *(inf.)* **indirizzo?**
kwal eh eel sooo / eel tooo eendeereet-tso

Here's my address / my email address.
Ecco il mio indirizzo / il mio indirizzo di posta elettronica.
ek-ko eel meeo eendeereet-tso / ... dee posta aylayt-troneeka

Giving your age

In Italian, you say how many years you <u>have</u> (**avere**), not how many years old you <u>are</u> (**essere**).

You'll find the numbers on the front cover flap.

How old are you?
Quanti anni ha *(formal)* **/ hai** *(inf.)***?**
kwantee an-nee a / I

I'm twenty years old.
Ho vent'anni.
o vayntan-nee

CONVERSING

I'm almost forty years old.
Ho quasi quarant'anni.
o **kwa**zee kwarantan-nee

We're the same age!
Siamo dunque coetanei!
s**ya**mo d**oo**nkweh koay**ta**nay

Talking about your family

When describing your marital status, remember to use the right form depending on whether you're a man or a woman.

I am ...	Sono...	**so**no
single.	**celibe, scapolo** *(m.)* / **nubile** *(f.)*.	che**lee**beh, **ska**polo / **noo**beeleh
married.	**sposato/-a.** *(m./f.)*	spo**za**to/-a
divorced.	**divorziato/-a.** *(m./f.)*	deevorts**ya**to/-a
a widow/widower.	**vedovo/-a.**	**ve**dovo/-a

To say who you're travelling with:

I'm here with ...	Sono qui con...	**so**no kwee kon
my husband.	**mio marito.**	**mee**o ma**ree**to
my wife.	**mia moglie.**	**mee**a **mo**lyeh
my parents.	**i miei genitori.**	ee **mee**ey jay**nee**toree
my father.	**mio padre.**	**mee**o **pa**dreh
my mother.	**mia madre.**	**mee**a **ma**dreh
my brother.	**mio fratello.**	**mee**o fra**tel**-lo
my sister.	**mia sorella.**	**mee**a so**rel**-la
my son.	**mio figlio.**	**mee**o **fee**lyo
my daughter.	**mia figlia.**	**mee**a **fee**lya

And if the conversation turns to children:

| Do you have children? | **Ha dei figli?** *(formal)* | a day **fee**lyee |
| I have two children. | **Ho due figli.** | o **doo**eh **fee**lyee |

| We have four children. | Abbiamo quattro figli. | ab-byamo kwat-tro feelyee |

We have...	Abbiamo...	ab-byamo
a boy.	un maschio.	oon maskyo
two (three, etc.) boys.	due (tre, etc.) maschi.	dooeh (treh) maskee
a girl.	una femmina.	oona fem-meena
two (three, etc.) girls.	due (tre, etc.) femmine.	dooeh (treh) fem-meeneh

Some other family members:

dad	papà	papa
mum	mamma	mam-ma
grandmother	nonna	non-na
grandfather	nonno	non-no
twins	gemelli/-e (m./f.)	jaymel-lee/-eh
infant	neonato	nayonato
baby	bimbo/-a (m./f.)	beembo/-a
adolescent/teenager	adolescente	adolayshenteh

Saying what you do

If you get onto the subject of what you do:

What's your job?
Che lavoro fai *(inf.)* **/ fa** *(formal)***?**
kay lavoro fI / fa

What are you studying?
Che cosa studi *(inf.)* **/ studia** *(formal)***?**
kay koza stoodee / stoodya

He/she is studying law.
Studia giurisprudenza.
stoodya jooreesproodentsa

Right now I'm looking for work.
Ora sto cercando lavoro.
ora sto chayrkando lavoro

In Italian, when saying what you do, there is no *a/an* – it's just **Sono** *I am* … or **Lavoro come** *I work as* … followed directly by the profession. In some cases, there is a different masculine and feminine form (indicated below in the order masc./fem.).

administrative employee	impiegato/-a amministrativo/-a	eempyaygato/-a am-meeneestrateevo/-a
architect	architetto	arkeetetto
baker	panettiere/-a	panayt-tyayreh/-a
bank employee	impiegato/-a di banca	eempyaygato/-a dee banka
childminder	assistente all'infanzia	asseestenteh al-leenfantsya
computer technician	informatico	eenformateeko
consultant	consulente	konsoolenteh
cook / chef	cuoco/-a	kwoko/-a
dentist	dentista	daynteesta
doctor	medico	medeeko
driver (bus, truck ~)	autista (di autobus, di camion)	aoteesta (dee aotoboos, dee kamyon)
engineer	ingegnere	eenjaynyayreh
farmer	agricoltore / agricoltrice	agreekoltoreh / agreekoltreecheh
firefighter	vigile del fuoco	veejeeleh del fwoko
gardener	giardiniere	jardeenyayreh
jeweller	gioielliere/-a	joyayl-lyayreh/-a

lawyer / solicitor	avvocato/-essa	av-vokato/-katayssa
nurse	infermiere/-a	eenfermyayreh/-a
painter (artist)	pittore/pittrice	peet-toreh/-treecheh
plumber	idraulico/-a	eedraoleeko/-a
police officer	poliziotto/-a	poleetsyot-to/-a
researcher	ricercatore / ricercatrice	reechayrkatoreh / reechayrkatreecheh
salesperson	commesso/-a	com-messo/-a
secretary	segretario/-a	saygraytaryo/-a
social worker	assistente sociale	asseestenteh sochaleh
student	studente/studentessa	stoodenteh/-dentayssa
taxi driver	tassista	tasseesta
teacher	maestro/-a	maaystro/-a
technician	tecnico	tekneeko
worker / labourer	operaio/-a	opayrayo/-a

Religion

The main religion in Italy is Roman Catholicism. The Vatican, the seat of the Roman Catholic Church, is in Rome. However, there is increasing diversity in religious beliefs and practices. As with professions, when giving your religion no *a/an* is used.

Are you practicing / observant?
Sei praticante? *(informal)*
sey prateekanteh

I am ...	Sono...	sono
agnostic.	agnostico/-a.	anyosteeko/-a
atheist.	ateo/-a.	atayo/-a
Buddhist.	buddista.	bood-deesta

Christian.	cristiano/-a.	kreest**ya**no/-a
Hindu.	induista.	eendoo**ee**sta
Jewish.	ebreo/-a.	e**bre**o/-a
Muslim.	musulmano/-a.	moozool**ma**no/-a
not religious.	senza religione.	**sen**tsa raylee**jo**neh
Orthodox.	ortodosso/-a.	orto**dos**so/-a
Protestant.	protestante.	protay**stan**teh
Shintoist.	scintoista.	sheento**ee**sta
Sikh.	sikh.	seek

The weather

Like anywhere, weather is a very popular topic of conversation. You can't go wrong with slipping in any of the following phrases.

What a beautiful day!	Che magnifica giornata!	kay man**yee**feeka jor**na**ta
It's so hot today!	Che caldo oggi!	kay **kal**do **oj**-jee
What horrible weather!	Che brutto tempo!	kay br**oot**-to **tem**po
It's so cold today!	Che freddo fa oggi!	kay **fred**-do fa **oj**-jee
It's windy.	Tira vento.	**tee**ra **ven**to

What's the forecast for tomorrow?	Quali sono le previsioni per domani?	**kwa**lee **so**no lay prayveez**yo**nee payr do**ma**nee
It will be nice.	Ci sarà bel tempo.	chee sa**ra** bel **tem**po
It's going to rain.	Pioverà.	pyovay**ra**

There is/are ... / There will be ...	C'è... / Ci sarà / saranno...	che / chee sa**ra** / sa**ran**-no
clouds.	le nuvole.	lay **noo**voleh
fog.	la nebbia.	la **neb**-bya

hail.	la grandine.	*la grandeeneh*
lightning.	i fulmini.	*ee foolmeenee*
rain.	la pioggia.	*la pyoj-ja*
snow.	la neve.	*la nayveh*
a storm.	una tempesta.	*oona tempesta*
sun.	il sole.	*eel soleh*
thunder.	i tuoni.	*ee twonee*
a thunderstorm.	un temporale.	*oon temporaleh*
wind.	il vento.	*eel vento*

Expressing opinions and feelings

If you're talking about something feminine in gender, remember to use the feminine form (ending in **-a**) with **Questa è...** Or to talk about more than one thing: **Questi/-e sono...**

It's ... (m./f.)	**Questo/-a è...**	*kwaysto/-a eh*
beautiful.	**bello/-a.**	*bel-lo/-a*
ugly.	**brutto/-a.**	*broot-to/-a*
amazing!	**stupendo/-a!**	*stoopendo/-a*
crazy!	**pazzesco/-a!**	*pat-tsaysko/-a*
extraordinary!	**straordinario/-a!**	*stra-ordeenaryo/-a*
horrible!	**spaventoso/-a!**	*spavayntozo/-a*
splendid!	**splendido/-a!**	*splendeedo/-a*
wonderful!	**meraviglioso/-a!**	*mayraveelyozo/-a*

In my opinion ...	**Secondo me...**	*saykondo may*
I like ...	**Mi piace...**	*mee pyacheh*
I don't like ...	**Non mi piace...**	*non mee pyacheh*
It's all the same to me.	**Fa lo stesso.**	*fa lo stesso*

CONVERSING

Here are some terms for expressing moods (remember to use the masculine or feminine form depending on the subject):

I am ... / He/she is ...	Sono... / è...	sono / eh
angry.	arrabbiato/-a.	arrab-byato/-a
down / depressed.	abbattuto/-a.	ab-bat-tooto/-a
frightened.	spaventato/-a.	spavayntato/-a
happy.	allegro/-a.	al-legro/-a
in tears.	in lacrime.	een lakreemeh
pleased.	contento/-a.	kontento/-a
proud.	fiero/-a.	fyayro/-a
sad.	triste/-a.	treesteh/-a
thoughtful / pensive.	pensoso/-a.	paynsozo/-a
unhappy.	scontento/-a.	skontento/-a

Invitations

Social life in Italy often revolves around eating and drinking – in piazzas, cafés, bars, restaurants or **a casa** *at home*. Here are some useful phrases if you're invited somewhere:

Can you come to dinner at our place this evening?
Verrebbe a cena da noi stasera? *(formal)*
vayrreb-beh a chayna da noy stasayra

Let's go to dinner this evening.
Andiamo a cena stasera.
andyamo a chayna stasayra

Can you come to dinner at our place tomorrow evening?
Verrebbe a cena da noi domani sera? *(formal)*
vayrreb-beh a chayna da noy domanee sayra

I hope that you'll be able to come.
Spero che Lei possa venire. *(formal)*
sp**ay**ro kay ley p**o**ssa vayn**ee**reh

Yes, I'd love to come.
Sì, verrò con piacere.
see vayrro kon pyach**ay**reh

I (m./f.) would be delighted to come, but tomorrow I can't.
Sarei lieto/-a di venire ma domani non posso.
sar**ey** ly**ay**to/-a dee vayn**ee**reh ma dom**a**nee non p**o**sso

I'm sorry I'm late.
Mi dispiace di essere in ritardo.
mee deespy**a**cheh dee **e**ssayreh een reet**a**rdo

You're too kind. Thank you so much!
Lei è troppo gentile. Grazie mille! *(formal)*
ley eh trop-po jaynt**ee**leh gr**a**tsyeh m**ee**l-leh

What time should we come?
A che ora dobbiamo venire?
a kay **o**ra dob-b**ya**mo vayn**ee**reh

Thank you for the wonderful evening. We've had a great time!
Grazie per la splendida serata. Ci siamo proprio divertiti!
gr**a**tsyeh payr la spl**e**nd**ee**da sayr**a**ta chee s**ya**mo pr**o**pryo deevayrt**ee**tee

Meeting up …

Italy is considered one of the most romantic places in the world. If you succumb, and the occasion presents itself, here are some trusty phrases for playing the game of seduction.

CONVERSING

Do you have a light?
Hai d'accendere, per favore?
I dachendayreh payr favoreh

Can I get you something to drink?
Posso offrirti qualcosa da bere?
posso of-freertee kwalkoza da bayreh

Is this your first time here?
È la prima volta che vieni qui?
eh la preema volta kay vyaynee kwee

This is the first time I've seen you here. You're not from here, are you?
È la prima volta che ti vedo qui. Non sei di queste parti vero?
eh la preema volta kay tee vaydo kwee non sey dee kwaysteh partee vayro

Are you waiting for someone?
Aspetti qualcuno?
aspet-tee kwalkoono

I'm not waiting for anyone.
Non aspetto nessuno.
non aspet-to nayssoono

Will we see each other tomorrow?
Ci vediamo domani?
chee vaydyamo domanee

... and chatting up

love	amore (m.)	amoreh
in love	innamorato/-a (m./f.)	een-namorato/-a
a kiss	un bacio	oon bacho
to kiss	baciarsi	bacharsee
to pick up	rimorchiare	reemorkyareh
to seduce / woo	sedurre / fare la corte	saydoorreh / fareh la korteh

| jealousy | **gelosia** (f.) | jaylozeea |
| quarrel / row | **scenata** (f.) | shaynata |

I like you. I'm crazy about you!
Mi piaci. Ti amo da impazzire!
mee pyachee tee amo da eempat-tseereh

I'm (m./f.) in love with you.
Sono innamorato/-a di te.
sono een-namorato/-a dee teh

Will you marry me?
Vuoi sposarmi?
vwoy spozarmee

You're the girl / the boy of my dreams!
Sei la ragazza / il ragazzo dei miei sogni!
sey la ragat-tsa / eel ragat-tso day meeey sonyee

⊿ Time and the calendar

Talking about time

In Italian, **il tempo** refers to *time* in a general sense (by the way, it also means *weather*!). To ask or give the time, **l'ora** *hour* is used. The 24-hour clock is common, especially in timetables, so don't be thrown by times from 13:00 to 24:00!

Telling the time

What time is it?
Che ora è?
kay ora eh

| It's a quarter past 11:00. | **Sono le undici e un quarto.** | sono lay oondeechee ay oon kwarto |
| It's 1:20. | **È l'una e venti.** | eh loona ay vayntee |

It's 2:25.	Sono le due e venticinque.	sono lay dooeh ay vaynteecheenkweh
It's 3:30.	Sono le tre e mezza.	sono lay treh ay med-dsa
It's twenty to six.	Sono le sei meno venti.	sono lay sey mayno vayntee
It's a quarter to seven.	Sono le sette meno un quarto.	sono lay set-teh mayno oon kwarto
It's five to seven.	Sono le sette meno cinque.	sono lay set-teh mayno cheenkweh
It's noon. / It's midnight.	È mezzogiorno. / È mezzanotte.	eh mayd-dsojorno / eh mayd-dsanot-teh

Notice that **sono** *they are* is used for times from 2:00–12:00.

Times of the day

morning	**mattina** (*f.*)	mat-teena
afternoon	**pomeriggio** (*m.*)	pomayreej-jo
evening	**sera** (*f.*)	sayra
night	**notte** (*f.*)	not-teh

'When' and 'how long'

At what time?	A che ora?	a kay ora
In 10 minutes.	Fra dieci minuti.	fra dyaychee meenootee
In a quarter of an hour.	Fra un quarto d'ora.	fra oon kwarto dora
In 45 minutes.	Fra tre quarti d'ora.	fra treh kwartee dora
In an hour.	Fra un'ora.	fra oonora
Half an hour ago.	Mezz'ora fa.	mayd-dsora fa

every half-hour	ogni mezz'ora	onyee mayd-dsora
every hour	ogni ora	onyee ora

It's early.	È presto.	eh presto
It's late.	È tardi.	eh tardee

| before / earlier | **prima** | *preema* |
| after / later | **dopo / più tardi** | *dopo / pyoo tardee* |

How long will it last?
Quanto tempo dura?
kwanto tempo doora

last / next Sunday	**domenica scorsa / prossima**	*domeneeka skorsa / prosseema*
last / next week	**la settimana scorsa / prossima**	*la sayt-teemana skorsa / prosseema*
last / next month	**il mese scorso / prossimo**	*eel mayzeh skorso / prosseemo*
last / next year	**l'anno scorso / prossimo**	*lan-no skorso / prosseemo*
this year	**quest'anno**	*kwaystan-no*
today	**oggi**	*oj-jee*
now	**ora / adesso**	*ora / adesso*
the day before yesterday	**l'altro ieri**	*laltro yayree*
tomorrow	**domani**	*domanee*
the day after tomorrow	**dopodomani**	*dopodomanee*
the next day	**l'indomani**	*leendomanee*
the day after	**il giorno dopo**	*eel jorno dopo*
ten days ago	**dieci giorni fa**	*dyaychee jornee fa*
in one week	**fra una settimana**	*fra oona sayt-teemana*

Days, months and seasons

The date is given using a cardinal number (i.e. 1, 2, 3, 4, etc.), followed by the month: **12 gennaio** *12 January* (refer to the cover flap for the numbers).

The days of the week and months are not capitalized.

CONVERSING

What day is it today?
Che giorno è oggi?
kay j**o**rno eh **o**j-jee

It's Tuesday, the 6th of July.
È martedì 6 luglio.
eh martayd**ee** sey l**oo**lyo

Days of the week

Monday	lunedì	loonaydee
Tuesday	martedì	martaydee
Wednesday	mercoledì	mayrkolaydee
Thursday	giovedì	jovaydee
Friday	venerdì	vaynayrdee
Saturday	sabato	sabato
Sunday	domenica	domayneeka

Months of the year

January	gennaio	jayn-nIo
February	febbraio	fayb-brIo
March	marzo	martso
April	aprile	apreeleh
May	maggio	maj-jo
June	giugno	joonyo
July	luglio	loolyo
August	agosto	agosto
September	settembre	sayt-tembreh
October	ottobre	ot-tobreh
November	novembre	novembreh
December	dicembre	deechembreh

Seasons

spring	**primavera** (f.)	preemavera
summer	**estate** (f.)	aystateh
autumn	**autunno** (m.)	aotoon-no
winter	**inverno** (m.)	eenverno

Festivals and holidays

Many of the national holidays (**giorni festivi** *[jornee faysteevee]*) in Italy are based on Roman Catholic religious festivals. Most businesses are closed on public holidays. The Italian-speaking area of Switzerland also celebrates many of these holidays. Those specific to one country or the other are indicated with (I) or (S).

1 January	*New Year* **Capodanno** *[capodan-no]*
6 January	*Epiphany* **Epifania** (**La Befana**) *[epeefaneea la bayfana]*: celebrates the visit of the Magi to the baby Jesus.
March–April	*Easter* **Pasqua** *[paskwa]* and *Easter Monday* **Lunedì dell'Angelo** *[loonaydee del-lanjaylo]*: celebrate the resurrection of Jesus Christ.
25 April	*Liberation Day* **Festa della Liberazione** *[festa del-la leebayratsyoneh]* (I): commemorates the end of the Nazi occupation of Italy in 1945.
1 May	*Labour Day* **Festa del lavoro** *[festa del lavoro]*
2 June	*Republic Day* **Festa della Repubblica Italiana** *[festa del-la raypoob-bleeka eetalyana]* (I): celebrates the day in 1946 when Italians voted to abolish the monarchy and become a republic.

CONVERSING

1 August	*Swiss National Day* **Festa nazionale svizzera** [festa natsyonaleh zveet-tsayra] (S): commemorates the founding in 1291 of the Swiss Confederation.
15 August	*Assumption Day* **Assunzione di Maria in Cielo** [assoontsyoneh dee mareea een chelo]: also called **Ferragosto** [fayrragosto], this day celebrates the Virgin Mary's ascension to heaven.
1 November	*All Saints' Day* **Ognissanti** [onyeessantee]: honours all the Catholic saints.
8 December	*Immaculate Conception* **Immacolata Concezione** [eem-makolata konchaytsyoneh]
24–25 December	*Christmas Eve* **Vigilia di Natale** [veejeelya dee nataleh] and *Christmas* **Natale** [nataleh]
26 December	*St Stephen's Day* **Santo Stefano** [santo stefano]: commemorates the first Christian martyr.
31 December	*New Year's Eve* **San Silvestro** [san seelvestro]: commemorates the death of Pope Sylvester I and the beginning of the new year.

↗ Asking for assistance

Emergencies

call for help	**richiesta** (f.) **di soccorso**	reek**yay**sta dee sok-**ko**rso
emergency	**emergenza** (f.)	aymayr**je**ntsa
medical aid	**primo soccorso** (m.)	**pree**mo sok-**ko**rso

In the event of an emergency, call the free European number (112) and they will put you through to the appropriate service.

Fire!	**Al fuoco!**	al f**wo**ko
Help!	**Aiuto!**	a**yoo**to
Watch out!	**Attenzione!**	atayntsyoneh

Call for help, quickly!
Chiamate *(pl.)* **aiuto presto!**
kyamateh ayooto presto

Call the police!
Chiami *(sing.)* **la polizia!**
kyamee la poleetseea

On the road

There has been an accident.
C'è stato un incidente.
che stato oon eencheedenteh

Don't move! (inf./formal)
Non muoverti / si muova!
non mwovertee / see mwova

Help is on its way.
Arrivano i soccorsi.
arreevano ee sok-korsee

↗ Signs, notices and abbreviations

Signs and notices

Here are some of the signs a wandering tourist is most likely to encounter:

Aperto / Chiuso	apayrto / kyoozo	Open / Closed
Cassa	kassa	Cash register / Till
È vietato...	eh vyaytato	No ... / Prohibited
Informazioni	informatsyonee	Information
Ingresso / Uscita	ingresso / oosheeta	Entrance / Exit
Libero / Occupato	leebayro / ok-koopato	Vacant / Occupied
Pericolo	payreekolo	Danger

Pericolo d'incendio	payreekolo deenchendyo	Fire hazard
Privato	preevato	Private
Riservato	reezayrvato	Reserved
Sala d'attesa	sala dat-teza	Waiting room
Saldi	saldee	Sale
Tirare / Spingere	teerareh / speenjayreh	Pull / Push
Toilette / Servizi	twalet / sayrveetsee	Toilets / Restrooms
Uomini (Servizi) / Donne (Servizi)	womeenee / don-neh (sayrveetsee)	Men's room / Women's room
Uscita di emergenza	oosheeta dee aymayrjentsa	Emergency exit
Vietato fumare	vyaytato foomareh	No smoking

Abbreviations

And a few common abbreviations:

a.C. (avanti Cristo)	BC/BCE (before Christ/Common Era)
a.D. (anno Domini)	AD/CE (Common Era)
ca. (circa)	circa
C.P. (casella postale)	post box
C.so. (Corso)	boulevard / street
d.C. (dopo Cristo)	AD/CE (Common Era)
E.N.I.T. (Ente Nazionale Italiano per il Turismo)	National Italian Office of Tourism
F.F.S. (Ferrovie Federali Svizzere)	Swiss Federal Railways
F.S. (Ferrovie dello Stato)	Italian State Railways
IVA (Imposta sul Valore Aggiunto)	VAT (value-added sales tax)
P.za (piazza)	square
RAI (Radio Audizioni Italiane)	Rai Italia (national public broadcaster)
sec. (secolo)	century
Sig. (Signor)	Mr

Sig.a (Signora)	Mrs
Sig.na (Signorina)	Miss
V.le (Viale)	avenue / boulevard

↗ Travelling

Passport control and customs

passport	**passaporto** *(m.)*	passaporto
passport control	**controllo** *(m.)* **dei passaporti**	kontrol-lo day passaportee
customs	**dogana** *(f.)*	dogana
nothing to declare	**nulla da dichiarare**	nool-la da deekyarareh
goods to declare	**merci da dichiarare**	merchee da deekyarareh
ID card	**carta** *(f.)* **d'identità**	karta deedaynteeta

I'm here ...	**Sono qui...**	sono kwee
on holiday.	in vacanza.	een vakantsa
to study.	per studio.	payr stoodyo
for work.	per lavoro.	payr lavoro

I'm sorry, I don't understand.
Mi scusi, non capisco. *(formal)*
mee skoozee non kapeesko

Is there someone here who speaks English?
C'è qualcuno qui che parla inglese?
che kwalkoono kwee kay parla eenglayzeh

I have nothing to declare.
Non ho nulla da dichiarare.
non o nool-la da deekyarareh

Money

Bank cards are widely used in Italy, but some smaller establishments prefer to be paid in cash.

Italian cards have a pin code; if your card doesn't, most businesses can swipe it.

Where is the nearest bureau de change?
Dov'è il cambio più vicino?
doveh eel kambyo pyoo veecheeno

I'd like to change ...	Vorrei cambiare...	vorrey kambyareh
some US dollars.	dei dollari americani.	day dol-laree amayreekanee
some Canadian dollars.	dei dollari canadesi.	day dol-laree kanadayzee
some Australian dollars.	dei dollari australiani.	day dol-laree aostralyanee
some New Zealand dollars.	dei dollari neozelandesi.	day dol-laree nayodsaylandayzee
some pounds sterling.	delle sterline britanniche.	del-leh stayrleeneh breetan-neekeh
some traveller's checks.	dei traveller's cheque.	day travayl-layrz shek

Flying

airline	compagnia (f.) aerea	kompanyeea aeraya
aisle	corridoio (m.)	korreedoyo
boarding pass	carta (f.) d'imbarco	karta deembarko
flight	volo (m.)	volo
layover	scalo (m.)	skalo
luggage	bagaglio (m.)	bagalyo
window (in a vehicle)	finestrino (m.)	feenestreeno

I would like to confirm (change / cancel) my reservation.
Vorrei confermare (cambiare / annullare) la mia prenotazione.
*vorr**ey** konfayrm**a**reh (kamb**ya**reh / an-nool-**la**reh) la m**ee**a praynotats**yo**neh*

What time does the plane leave?
A che ora decolla l'aereo?
*a kay **o**ra dayk**o**l-la la**e**rayo*

What time does the plane arrive?
A che ora atterra l'aereo?
*a kay **o**ra at-t**e**rra la**e**rayo*

What is the latest check-in time?
Qual è il tempo limite di accettazione / di check-in?
*kwal eh eel t**e**mpo l**ee**meeteh dee ach**a**yt-tats**yo**neh / dee chek**ee**n*

Where is boarding gate 2?
Dove si trova la porta d'imbarco n° 2?
*d**o**veh see tr**o**va la p**o**rta deemb**a**rco n**oo**mayro d**oo**eh*

Going by bus or train

Where is the (railway) station?
Dove si trova la stazione (ferroviaria)?
*d**o**veh see tr**o**va la stats**yo**neh (fayrrov**ya**rya)*

From which platform does the train going to ... leave?
Da che binario parte il treno per...?
*da kay been**a**ryo p**a**rteh eel tr**a**yno payr*

Is the train late?
È in ritardo il treno?
*eh een reet**a**rdo eel tr**a**yno*

Is there a strike?
C'è uno sciopero?
*che **oo**no shop**a**yro*

CONVERSING

The train is ten minutes late.
Il treno è in ritardo di dieci minuti.

eel trayno eh een reetardo dee dyaychee meenootee

dining/restaurant car	**carrozza** (f.) **bar-ristorante**	karrot-tsa bar reestoranteh
sleeping car	**carrozza** (f.) **letti**	karrot-tsa let-tee
ticket inspector	**controllore** (m.)	kontrol-loreh
reservation	**prenotazione** (f.)	praynotatsyoneh

Is this the train ...	È questo il treno...	eh kwaysto eel trayno
going to Bari?	**per Bari?**	payr baree
going to Genoa?	**per Genova?**	payr jenova
going to Milan?	**per Milano?**	payr meelano
going to Naples?	**per Napoli?**	payr napolee
going to Rome?	**per Roma?**	payr roma
going to Turin?	**per Torino?**	payr toreeno
going to Venice?	**per Venezia?**	payr vaynetsya

Is it a direct train?
È un treno diretto?

eh oon trayno deeret-to

Is this seat free?
È libero quel posto?

eh leebayro kwayl posto

What time will we arrive in ...?
A che ora arriveremo a...?

a kay ora arreevayraymo a

I'm getting off at the next stop.
Scendo alla prossima fermata.

shendo al-la prosseema fayrmata

If you're travelling by bus, just replace **il treno** *train* in the preceding phrases with **il pullman** *[eel pool-lman]* or **la corriera** *[la korryayra] long-distance bus, coach.*

Where is the bus/coach station?
Dove si trova la stazione dei pullman / delle corriere?
doveh see trova la statsyoneh day pool-lman / del-leh korryayreh

Where is the bus/coach stop?
Dove si trova la fermata dei pullman / delle corriere?
doveh see trova la fayrmata day pool-lman / del-leh korryayreh

Is this the right direction to go to ... ?
È questa la direzione giusta per andare a...?
eh kwaysta la deeraytsyoneh joosta payr andareh a

When does the first / next / last bus/coach for ... leave?
A che ora parte la prima / la prossima / l'ultima corriera per...?
a kay ora parteh la preema / la prosseema / loolteema korryayra payr

Is there a connection to ... ? What time does it leave?
C'è una coincidenza per...? A che ora parte?
che oona ko-eencheedentsa payr... a kay ora parteh

Where is the timetable/schedule?
Dov'è l'orario?
doveh loraryo

How long is the journey?
Quanto tempo dura il percorso?
kwanto tempo doora eel payrkorso

Buying a ticket

Where is the ticket counter?
Dov'è lo sportello?
dov**eh** lo sport**el**-lo

How much does a ticket to … cost?
Quanto costa il biglietto per…?
kwanto **ko**sta eel beel**yay**t-to payr

I would like a …	Vorrei un biglietto…	vor**rey** oon beel**yay**t-to
return ticket for …	andata e ritorno per…	an**da**ta ay ree**tor**no payr
one-way ticket for …	andata per…	an**da**ta payr
half-price ticket	a metà prezzo	a **may**ta pret-tso

Is it possible to get an e-ticket?
È possibile emettere un biglietto elettronico?
eh pos**see**beeleh aym**et**-tayreh oon beel**yay**t-to aylayt-tr**o**neeko

Going by boat

Italy has a lot of coastline and numerous islands (the largest of these are Sardinia and Sicily). There are many ferry services linking destinations along the coast or offshore.

boat / ship	**nave** (f.)	**na**veh
arrival	**arrivo** (m.)	ar**ree**vo
departure	**partenza** (f.)	par**ten**tsa
cabin with 4 beds	**cabina** (f.) **con 4 posti letto**	ka**bee**na kon **kwa**t-tro **pos**tee **let**-to
journey / route	**percorso** (m.)	payr**kor**so
line	**linea** (f.)	**lee**naya

passenger	passeggero/-a	passayj-jayro/-a
port agency	agenzia (f.) portuale / agenzia (f.) marittima	ajentseea portwaleh / ajentseea mareet-teema
reservation	prenotazione (f.)	praynotatsyoneh
reserved seat	poltrona (f.)	poltrona
ticket	biglietto (m.)	beelyayt-to
ticket office	biglietteria (f.)	beelyayt-tereea
free (of charge)	gratuito	gratooeeto
50% discount	50% di sconto	cheenkwanta payrchento dee skonto

Going by taxi

All Italian taxis are required to use a meter. The price is higher between midnight and 5 a.m. Also note that there is a higher pick-up charge from an airport. Tipping is not expected.

Where can I find a taxi?
Dove posso trovare un taxi?
doveh posso trovareh oon taksee

Take me to the hotel ... / to the station, please.
Mi porti all'albergo... / alla stazione, per favore.
mee portee al-lalbayrgo… / al-la statsyoneh payr favoreh

Here's the address, thank you.
Ecco l'indirizzo, grazie.
ek-ko leendeereet-tso gratsyeh

Go straight ahead.
Vada sempre dritto.
vada sempreh dreet-to

This is fine, you can stop here.
Va bene, si fermi qui.
va beneh see fermee kwee

CONVERSING

I'll walk from here.
Proseguo a piedi.
pros*e*gwo a p*yay*dee

How much do I owe you?
Quanto Le devo?
k*wa*nto lay d*ay*vo

Do you take credit cards?
Accetta la carta di credito?
ach*e*t-ta la k*a*rta dee kr*e*deeto

Biking and motorcycling

In some places you can rent a moped for doing some sightseeing in the local countryside or for getting around town.

bicycle	**bicicletta** (f.)	beecheeklet-ta
motorcycle	**moto** (f.)	moto
moped / motor-scooter	**scooter** (m.)	sk*oo*tayr

Renting a car

I would like to rent a car for the week / the weekend.
Vorrei noleggiare una macchina per una settimana / il fine settimana.
vorr*ey* nolayj-jareh **oo**na mak-keena payr **oo**na sayt-teemana / eel f*ee*neh sayt-teemana

Driving

In Italy, most **autostrade** *motorways/freeways* are toll roads. At **il pedaggio** *the tollgate*, avoid the lane marked 'Telepass' as this is reserved for an automatic payment system. Distances and speeds are given in kilometres: the maximum speed on most motorways is 130 km/h (about 80 mph).

Where is the nearest gas/petrol station?
Dov'è la stazione di servizio più vicina?
*dov**eh** la stats**yo**neh dee sayrv**ee**tsyo pyoo veech**ee**na*

I would like 20 litres* of premium unleaded, please.
Vorrei venti litri di Super senza piombo, per favore.
*vor**rey** v**e**ntee l**ee**tree dee s**oo**payr s**e**ntsa p**yo**mbo payr fav**o**reh*

*There are almost 4 litres in a gallon.

A full tank, please.
Il pieno, per piacere.
*eel p**yay**no payr pyach**ay**reh*

Problems

If you need help:

Where is the nearest garage?
Dov'è il garage più vicino?
*dov**eh** eel gar**a**ge* pyoo veech**ee**no*

* This is a loanword, so it doesn't follow regular pronunciation rules: the **ge** is pronounced as in 'beige'.

Can you check the tire pressure?
Potete controllare la pressione delle gomme?
*pot**ay**teh kontrol-l**a**reh la prayss**yo**neh d**e**l-leh g**o**m-meh*

I need to change this tire.
Bisogna sostituire questa gomma.
*beez**o**nya sosteetoo**ee**reh k**way**sta g**o**m-ma*

CONVERSING

My car has broken down.
Ho un guasto alla macchina.
o oon gwasto al-la mak-keena

This doesn't work.
Questo non funziona.
kwaysto non foontsyona

How much time will it take to repair it?
Quanto tempo ci vorrà per ripararla?
kwanto tempo chee vorra payr reepararla

I would like to know how much this repair is going to cost.
Vorrei sapere quanto viene a costare questa riparazione.
vorrey sapayreh kwanto vyayneh a kostareh kwaysta reeparatsyoneh

And if someone has offered you a hand:

Thank you so much for your help!
Grazie mille per l'aiuto!
gratsyeh meel-leh payr layooto

Useful words

back / rear	**dietro** *(m.)*	*dyaytro*
battery	**batteria** *(f.)*	*bat-tayreea*
brakes	**freni** *(m.)*	*frenee*
clutch	**frizione** *(f.)*	*freetsyoneh*
contact	**contatto** *(m.)*	*kontat-to*
diesel	**diesel** *(m.)*	*deezel*
direction	**direzione** *(f.)*	*deeraytsyoneh*
driver's licence	**patente** *(f.)*	*patenteh*
front	**davanti** *(m.)*	*davantee*
gas / petrol	**benzina** *(f.)*	*bayndseena*
headlight	**faro** *(m.)*	*faro*
ignition	**accensione** *(f.)*	*achaynsyoneh*

insurance	**assicurazione** (f.)	asseekoorats**yo**neh
light bulbs	**lampadine** (f.)	lampad**ee**neh
lights	**luci** (f.)	**loo**chee
motor	**motore** (m.)	mot**o**reh
pedal	**pedale** (m.)	payd**a**leh
safety vest (with reflective stripes)	**gilet** (m.) **di sicurezza (con strisce rifrangenti)**	jeel**eh** dee seekoor**et**-tsa (kon str**ee**sheh reefranj**en**tee)
seatbelt	**cintura** (f.) **di sicurezza**	cheent**oo**ra dee seekoor**et**-tsa
snow chains	**catene** (f.) **da neve**	kat**e**neh da n**e**veh
spark plugs	**candele** (f.)	kand**e**leh
starter	**starter** (m.)	st**a**rtayr
wheels	**ruote** (f.)	r**wo**teh
windscreen wipers	**tergicristalli** (m.)	tayrjeekreest**a**l-lee

fine	**multa** (f.)	m**oo**lta
motorway / freeway	**autostrada** (f.)	aotostr**a**da
parking	**parcheggio** (m.)	park**ayj**-jo
toll / tollgate	**pedaggio** (m.)	payd**aj**-jo

Some common road signs

Alt	alt	Stop
Attenzione	at-tents**yo**neh	Caution
Deviazione	dayvyats**yo**neh	Diversion / Detour
Fermata	fayrm**a**ta	Bus stop
Fine	f**ee**neh	End
Lavori	lav**o**ree	Roadworks
Limitazione di altezza	leemeetats**yo**neh dee altet-tsa	Low clearance
Pericolo	payr**ee**kolo	Danger
Senso unico	senso **oo**neeko	One way

Senza uscita	sentsa oosheeta	No exit / Dead end
Vietato	vyaytato	Prohibited / Keep out
Velocità controllata elettronicamente	velocheeta kontrol-lata aylayt-troneekamenteh	Speed monitored by radar

↗ Getting around town

Finding your way around

How can I get to ...?
Come posso andare a...?
komeh posso andareh a

Is there a bus going to ...?
C'è un autobus per...?
che oon aotoboos payr

It's ...	È...	eh
to the left.	a sinistra.	a seeneestra
to the right.	a destra.	a destra
to the north.	verso nord.	verso nord
to the south.	verso sud.	verso sood
to the east.	verso est.	verso est
to the west.	verso ovest.	verso ovayst

Where is ...	Dove si trova...	doveh see trova
... street?	la via...?	la veea
... square?	la piazza...?	la pyat-tsa
the ... building?	l'edificio...?	laydeefeecho

Taking public transport

Cities such as Rome, Milan and Genoa have underground train networks – **il metrò** [eel metro] (m.) or **la metro** [la metro] (f.). Venice has a unique public transport system based on **vaporettos** ('water buses') that run along the main waterways.

Where is the nearest metro station?
Dov'è la stazione della metro più vicina?
doveh la statsyoneh del-la metro pyoo veecheena

What line is this?
Che linea è questa?
kay leenaya eh kwaysta

What line should I take to go to ...	Che linea devo prendere per...	kay leenaya dayvo prendayreh payr
the centre of town?	... il centro città?	eel chentro cheet-ta
the airport?	... l'aeroporto?	la-ayroporto or larayoporto
the port?	... il porto?	eel porto
the Colosseum / the Roman Forum?	... il Colosseo / i Fori imperiali?	eel kolossayo / ee foree eempayryalee
the cathedral?	... il Duomo?	eel dwomo
the central station?	... la stazione centrale?	la statsyoneh chayntraleh

Is there a direct line or do I need to change?
C'è una linea diretta o devo cambiare?
che oona leenaya deeret-ta o dayvo kambyareh

The next train / metro is in five minutes.
Il prossimo treno / La prossima metropolitana arriva fra cinque minuti.
eel prosseemo trayno / la prosseema maytropoleetana arreeva fra cheenkweh meenootee

What time does the last connection leave?
A che ora parte l'ultima coincidenza?
a kay ora parteh loolteema ko-eencheedentsa

CONVERSING

Sites and places of interest

With its 50 UNESCO World Heritage Sites, Italy is teeming with archaeology, history, architecture and art. From north to south, the country is exceptionally rich in cultural treasures.

abbey	**abbazia** (f.)	ab-batsɜea
archaeological site (excavation)	**sito** (m.) **archeologico** (**scavi**)	seeto arkayolojeeko (skavee)
castle	**castello** (m.)	kastel-lo
cathedral	**cattedrale** (f.)	kat-taydraleh
church	**chiesa** (f.)	kyayza
exhibition	**mostra** (f.)	mostra
fortress	**fortezza** (f.)	fortet-tsa
monastery	**monastero** (m.)	monastayro
mosque	**moschea** (f.)	moskaya
museum	**museo** (m.)	moozayo
palace	**palazzo** (m.)	palat-tso
synagogue	**sinagoga** (f.)	seenagoga
temple	**tempio** (m.)	tempyo
tower	**torre** (f.)	torreh

Some tourist sites offer guided visits.

Is there a guide who speaks English?
C'è una guida che parla inglese?
che oona gweeda kay parla inglayzeh

The children are under the age of 10.
I bambini hanno meno di dieci anni.
ee bambeenee an-no meno dee dyaychee an-nee

Can we take photos?
Si possono fare foto?
see possono fareh foto

I would like a ticket ...	Vorrei un biglietto...	vorrey oon beelyayt-to
for one adult.	per un adulto.	payr oon adoolto
for two adults.	per due adulti.	payr dooeh adooltee
for two children.	per due bambini.	payr dooeh bambeenee
for a student.	per studente.	payr stoodenteh

Where is/are ...	Dove si trova / trovano...	doveh see trova / trovano
the aquarium?	l'acquario?	lakwaryo
the art gallery?	la galleria d'arte?	la gal-layreea darteh
the botanical garden?	il giardino botanico?	eel jardeeno botaneeko
the cemetery?	il cimitero?	eel cheemeetero
the fountain?	la fontana?	la fontana
the market?	il mercato?	eel mayrkato
the park?	il parco?	eel parko
the port?	il porto?	eel porto
the ruins?	le rovine?	lay roveeneh
the stadium?	lo stadio?	lo stadyo

Posting a letter

The Italian postal service is called **Poste Italiane** *[posteh eetalyaneh]* – you can spot post offices by their yellow and blue signs. Postboxes are small and red and are usually found attached to the wall near a **tabaccheria** *tobacconist's*, where you can also buy stamps, and often, postcards.

CONVERSING

Where is the nearest post office?
Dov'è l'ufficio postale più vicino?
*dov**eh** loof-**fee**cho post**a**leh pyoo veech**ee**no*

I would like some stamps for the UK / Canada / Australia / New Zealand / the United States, please.
Vorrei dei francobolli per il Regno Unito / il Canada / l'Australia / la Nuova Zelanda / gli Stati Uniti, per favore.
*vorr**ey** day frankob**o**l-lee payr eel **ray**nyo oon**ee**to / eel k**a**nada / laostr**a**lya / la **nwo**va dsayl**a**nda / lyee st**a**tee oon**ee**tee payr fav**o**reh*

I would like to mail this package to the UK / Canada / Australia / New Zealand / the United States, please.
Vorrei spedire questo pacco nel Regno Unito / in Canada / in Australia / in Nuova Zelanda / negli Stati Uniti, per favore.
*vorr**ey** spayd**ee**reh **kway**sto pak-ko nel **ray**nyo oon**ee**to / een k**a**nada / een aostr**a**lya / een **nwo**va dsayl**a**nda / **nel**yee st**a**tee oon**ee**tee payr fav**o**reh*

I would like to send a letter / a postcard.
Vorrei spedire una lettera / una cartolina.
*vorr**ey** spayd**ee**reh **oo**na l**ayt**-tera / **oo**na kartol**ee**na*

I would like to send a letter by registered post.
Vorrei spedire una lettera raccomandata.
*vorr**ey** spayd**ee**reh **oo**na l**ayt**-tera rak-komand**a**ta*

Making a phone call

When calling land lines, the first zero in the number must be included, even when calling internationally. (Mobile phone numbers don't start with zero, but with 3.)

I have to make a call.
Devo fare una telefonata.
dayvo fareh oona taylayfonata

Can I speak to Marco?
Posso parlare a Marco?
posso parlareh a marko

Hello? Good morning, I'd like to speak to Antonella.
Pronto? Buongiorno, vorrei parlare con Antonella.
pronto bwonjorno vorrey parlareh kon antonel-la

I'm sorry, I dialled the wrong number.
Mi dispiace, ho sbagliato numero.
mee deespyacheh o zbalyato noomayro

The line is busy/engaged.
La linea è occupata.
la leenaya eh ok-koopata

area code	**prefisso** (m.) **telefonico**	prayfeesso taylayfoneeko
phone booth/box	**cabina** (f.) **telefonica**	kabeena taylayfoneeka
prepaid card	**tessera** (f.) **prepagata**	tessayra praypagata

Going online

To access an establishment's wifi, just ask for **il nome della rete** *the name of the network* and **la password**.

CPU (Central Processing Unit)	**unità** (f.) **centrale**	ooneeta chayntraleh
email address	**indirizzo** (m.) **email**	eendeereet-tso eemayl
high-speed	**alto debito**	alto debeeto
internet access	**accesso** (m.) **Internet**	achesso eentayrnayt

CONVERSING

laptop	**computer** (m.) **portatile**	kompyootayr portateeleh
social networks	**reti** (f.) **sociali**	retee sochalee
web page	**pagina** (f.) **web**	pajeena wayb
wireless / wifi	**Wi-Fi** (m.)	wI fI

Where can I find an internet café or a free wifi zone?
Dove posso trovare un Internet cafè o una zona wi-fi gratuita?
doveh posso trovareh oon eentayrnayt kafeh o oona dsona wI fI gratooeeta

Internet access costs 4 euros for 1 hour.
Il costo della connessione è 4 euro all'ora.
eel kosto del-la kon-nayssyoneh eh kwat-tro ayooro al-lora

Excuse me, my headphones aren't working.
Scusi, la mia cuffia non funziona
skoozee la meea koof-fya non foontsyona

How much is it to print out a page?
Quanto costa stampare una pagina?
kwanto kosta stampareh oona pajeena

Administration and forms

Hopefully you'll be able to avoid bureaucratic tasks, but if not:

What are your opening hours?
Quali sono gli orari di apertura?
kwalee sono lyee oraree dee apayrtoora

What documents do I need to bring?
Quali documenti devo portare?
kwalee dokoomentee dayvo portareh

You need to go to counter 5 with the following documents.
Lei deve presentarsi allo sportello n°5 munito dei seguenti documenti.
ley dayveh prayzayntarsee al-lo sportel-lo noomayro cheenkweh mooneeto day saygwayntee dokoomentee

You need to fill out this form.
Lei deve compilare questo modulo.
ley dayveh kompeelareh kwaysto modoolo

I made a mistake.
Mi sono sbagliato.
mee sono zbalyato

Reporting a theft or loss

Where's the police station, please?
Dov'è la stazione di polizia, per favore?
doveh la statsyoneh dee poleetseea payr favoreh

Someone has stolen ...	Mi hanno rubato...	mee an-no roobato
my bank card.	il bancomat.	eel bankomat
my handbag.	la borsa.	la borsa
my mobile/cell phone.	il cellulare.	eel chayl-loolareh
my papers. (ID)	i documenti.	ee dokoomentee
my suitcase.	la valigia.	la valeeja
my wallet.	il portafoglio.	eel portafolyo

At the bank

An ATM (cash machine) is a **bancomat**. They are easy to find. Banks are typically open Monday to Friday from 8:30 to 1:30 and then after lunch from 3:00 to 4:00.

CONVERSING

Can you tell me where the nearest bank is?
Sa dirmi dov'è la banca più vicina?
sa d**ee**rmee dov**eh** la b**a**nka pyoo veech**ee**na

Where can I find an ATM?
Dove posso trovare un bancomat?
d**o**veh p**o**sso trov**a**reh oon b**a**nkomat

I'm waiting for a transfer from England / the United States.
Sto aspettando un bonifico dall'Inghilterra / dagli Stati Uniti.
sto aspayt-t**a**ndo oon bon**ee**feeko dal-leenghe**e**lterra / d**a**lyee st**a**tee oon**ee**tee

I would like to make a bank transfer – what should I do?
Vorrei fare un bonifico, come devo fare?
vorr**ey** f**a**reh oon bon**ee**feeko k**o**meh d**a**yvo f**a**reh

Going to a performance

Italy has many historic opera houses, theatres and concert halls. There is also a strong tradition of filmmaking. Note that most foreign films are dubbed: to see the original version with Italian subtitles, look for films marked **lingua originale**.

What's showing at the cinema this evening?
Cosa danno al cinema stasera?
k**o**za d**a**n-no al ch**ee**nayma stas**a**yra

What's on ...	Che cosa c'è...	kay k**o**za che
at the National Theatre?	al Teatro Nazionale?	al tay**a**tro natsyon**a**leh
at the Phoenix Theatre?	al Teatro La Fenice?	al tay**a**tro la fayn**ee**cheh
at the Scala?	alla Scala?	al-la sk**a**la

What time does the performance start?
A che ora inizia lo spettacolo?
a kay ora eeneetsya lo spayt-takolo

What time does it end?
A che ora finisce?
a kay ora feeneesheh

Where is the concert hall?
Dov'è la sala da concerto?
doveh la sala da konchayrto

Is there a nice bar nearby?
C'è un bar simpatico qui vicino?
che oon bar seempateeko kwee veecheeno

Is there a dance club nearby?
C'è una discoteca qui vicino?
che oona deeskoteka kwee veecheeno

At the hairdresser's

A hairdresser or *barber* is **un parrucchiere**. It's usually wise to make **una seduta** *an appointment*.

I would like a haircut.
Vorrei un taglio.
vorrey oon talyo

I would like ...	Vorrei...	vorrey
my hair dyed.	fare il colore.	fareh eel koloreh
a fringe/bangs.	la frangia.	la franja

I would like my hair ...	Vorrei i capelli...	vorrey ee kapel-lee
darker.	più scuri.	pyoo skooree
lighter.	più chiari.	pyoo kyaree
blond.	biondi.	byondee
black.	neri.	nayree
brown.	castani.	kastanee
the same colour.	dello stesso colore.	del-lo stesso koloreh
wavy.	ondulati.	ondoolatee

A short haircut, please.
Un taglio corto, per piacere.
oon talyo korto payr pyachayreh

Not too short, but a little more.
Non troppo corti, ma ancora un po'.
non trop-po kortee ma ankora oon po

It's perfect like that.
Va bene così.
va beneh kozee

↗ Outdoor activities

Recreation

To say you practice a sport or activity, just put the verb **fare** *to do* before the noun, e.g. **fare surf** *surfing*.

bike	**bici** (f.)	beechee
horseback riding	**equitazione** (f.)	aykweetatsyoneh
rock climbing	**arrampicata** (f.)	arrampeekata
rollerblades	**roller** (m.)	rol-layr

running	**corsa** (f.) **a piedi**	k**o**rsa a p**yay**dee
sled	**slitta** (f.)	zl**ee**t-ta
snowboard	**snowboard** (m.)	zn**o**bord
surfboard	**surf** (m.)	serf
windsurfing board	**windsurf** (m.)	w**ee**ndserf

For enthusiasts of **escursionismo** *[eskoorsyoneezmo] hiking*:

How far are we from …?
Quanto siamo lontani da…?
k**wa**nto s**ya**mo lont**a**nee da

How far is the next village?
Quanto dista il paese più vicino?
k**wa**nto d**ee**sta eel pa**ay**zeh pyoo veech**ee**no

bridge	**ponte** (m.)	p**o**nteh
canal	**canale** (m.)	kan**a**leh
cliff	**scogliera** (f.)	skoly**ay**ra
farm	**fattoria** (f.)	fat-tor**ee**a
ferry	**traghetto** (m.)	trag**ay**t-to
field	**campo** (m.)	k**a**mpo
forest	**foresta** (f.)	for**e**sta
hamlet	**borgo** (m.)	b**o**rgo
hill	**collina** (f.)	kol-l**ee**na
house	**casa** (f.)	k**a**za
inn / lodging	**locanda** (f.)	lok**a**nda
lake	**lago** (m.)	l**a**go
mountain	**montagna** (f.)	mont**a**nya
mountain chain	**catena** (f.) **montuosa**	kat**e**na montoo**o**za
path	**cammino** (m.)	kam-m**ee**no
peak	**picco** (m.)	p**ee**k-ko

pond	**stagno** (m.)	stanyo
river	**fiume** (m.)	fyoomeh
road	**strada** (f.)	strada
source / spring	**sorgente** (f.)	sorjenteh
trail / path	**sentiero** (m.)	sayntyero
tree	**albero** (m.)	albayro
valley	**valle** (f.)	val-leh
village	**paese** (m.)	paayzeh
vineyard	**vigneto** (m.)	veenyayto
waterfall	**cascata** (f.)	kaskata
waterway	**corso** (m.) **d'acqua**	korso dakwa
well	**pozzo** (m.)	pot-tso

For vocabulary about hiking equipment, refer to the end of the 'Camping' section (pages 106–107).

At the pool or beach

To swim is **nuotare**; *to go for a swim* is **fare il bagno**.

Is there an (outdoor / indoor) pool nearby?
C'è una piscina (all'aperto / coperta) qui vicino?
che **oo**na peesh**ee**na (al-laperto / koperta) kwee veech**ee**no

Is it heated?
È riscaldata?
eh reeskald**a**ta

How much is the entry fee?
Quanto costa l'ingresso?
kw**a**nto k**o**sta leengresso

Is there a sandy beach nearby?
C'è una spiaggia di sabbia qui vicino?
che **oo**na sp**ya**j-ja dee s**a**b-bya kwee veech**ee**no

I would like to rent ...	Vorrei noleggiare...	vorrey nolayj-jareh
a beach chair.	una sdraio.	**oo**na zdr**I**o
a beach umbrella.	un ombrellone.	oon ombrel-**lo**neh
a surfboard.	una tavola da surf.	**oo**na ta**v**ola da serf

How much is a two-hour rental?
Quanto costa il noleggio per due ore?
k**wa**nto k**o**sta eel nol**ay**j-jo payr d**oo**eh **o**reh

Camping

Can we camp here?
Si può campeggiare qui?
see pwo kampej-j**a**reh kwee

Is there a campsite nearby?
C'è un campeggio qui vicino?
che oon kamp**ej**-jo kwee veech**ee**no

Is it possible to make a fire?
È possibile accendere un fuoco?
eh poss**ee**beeleh ach**e**ndayreh oon f**wo**ko

What is the price ...	Qual è il prezzo...	kwal eh eel pret-tso
per day?	al giorno?	al j**o**rno
per person?	per persona?	payr payrs**o**na
for a car?	per una macchina?	payr **oo**na mak-k**ee**na
for a tent?	per una tenda?	payr **oo**na t**e**nda
for a caravan/trailer?	per una roulotte?	payr **oo**na rool**o**t
for a camping van?	per un camper?	payr oon kamp**ay**r

CONVERSING

Here are some terms for camping and hiking equipment:

backpack / rucksack	zaino (m.)	dsIno
bucket	secchio (m.)	sek-kyo
camp bed	brandina (f.)	brandeena
camping chairs	sedie (f.) da campeggio	sedyeh da kampej-jo
camping van	camper (m.)	kampayr
compass	bussola (f.)	boossola
cooler	frigorifero (m.) da campeggio	freegoreefayro da kampej-jo
corkscrew	cavatappi (m.)	kavatap-pee
extension cables/cords	prolunghe (f.) elettriche	proloongheh aylet-treekeh
first-aid kit	borsa (f.) del pronto soccorso	borsa del pronto sok-korso
flashlight / torch	torcia (f.) elettrica	torcha aylet-treeka
gas canister	ricambi (m.) gas	reekambee gas
glasses (drinking ~)	bicchieri (m.)	beek-kyayree
hammer	martello (m.)	martel-lo
kettle	bollitore (m.)	bol-leetoreh
lighting	illuminazione (f.)	il-loomeenatsyoneh
mat	stuoia (f.)	stwoya
matches	fiammiferi (m.)	fyam-meefayree
mattress (foam ~)	materasso (m.) di spugna	matayrasso dee spoonya
mattress (inflatable ~)	materassino (m.) gonfiabile	matayrasseeno gonfyabeeleh
mess tin (scout's ~)	gavetta (f.) scout	gavet-ta skowt
mosquito net / screen	zanzariera (f.)	dsandsaryayra
opener (bottle ~)	apribottiglie (m.)	apreebot-teelyeh
opener (can/tin ~)	apriscatole (m.)	apreeskatoleh
pan (frying ~)	padella (f.)	padel-la
pots	pentole (f.)	pentoleh

pumps	pompe (f.) / gonfiatori (m.)	pompeh / gonfyatoree
rope / cable	corda (f.)	korda
screwdriver	cacciavite (m.)	kachaveeteh
sleeping bag	sacco (m.) a pelo	sak-ko a pelo
sleeping bag (thermal ~)	borsa (f.) termica	borsa termeeka
stove (gas camping ~)	fornelletto (m.) a gas	fornel-let-to a gas
table (folding ~)	tavolino (m.) (pieghevole)	tavoleeno (pyaygayvoleh)
tarpaulin	telone (m.)	tayloneh
tent	tenda (f.)	tenda
tent stakes/pegs	picchetti (m.) di tenda	peek-ket-tee dee tenda
thermos	thermos (m.)	tayrmos
toilets (portable ~)	toilettes (f.) portatili	twalet portateelee
water bottle / flask	borraccia (f.)	borracha

Trees and plants

Trees

almond	mandorlo (m.)	mandorlo
beech	faggio (m.)	faj-jo
chestnut	castagno (m.)	kastanyo
cypress	cipresso (m.)	cheepresso
eucalyptus	eucalipto (m.)	ayookaleepto
fig	fico (m.)	feeko
fir	abete (m.)	abayteh
holm oak	leccio (m.)	laycho
lemon	limone (m.)	leemoneh
mulberry	gelso (m.)	jelso
oak	rovere (f.)	rovayreh
olive	ulivo (m.)	ooleevo
orange	arancio (m.)	arancho

CONVERSING

pine	**pino** *(m.)*	*peeno*
plane	**platano** *(m.)*	*platano*
pomegranate	**melograno** *(m.)*	*maylograno*
(weeping) willow	**salice** *(m.)* **(piangente)**	*saleecheh pyanjenteh*

Plants and shrubs

acanthus	**acanto** *(m.)*	*akanto*
basil	**basilico** *(m.)*	*bazeeleeko*
bougainvillea	**bougainvillea** *(f.)*	*booganveel-laya*
broom (Scotch ~)	**ginestra** *(f.)*	*jeenestra*
cactus	**cactus** *(m.)*	*kaktoos*
hibiscus	**ibisco** *(m.)*	*eebeesko*
jasmine	**gelsomino** *(m.)*	*jaylsomeeno*
juniper	**ginepro** *(m.)*	*jeenaypro*
lavender	**lavanda** *(f.)*	*lavanda*
mimosa	**mimosa** *(f.)*	*meemoza*
myrtle	**mirto** *(m.)*	*meerto*
oleander	**oleandro** *(m.)*	*olayandro*
oregano	**origano** *(m.)*	*oreegano*
rosemary	**rosmarino** *(m.)*	*rosmareeno*
thyme	**timo** *(m.)*	*teemo*

Animals

Mammals

bat	**pipistrello** *(m.)*	*peepeestrel-lo*
bear	**orso** *(m.)*	*orso*
dolphin	**delfino** *(m.)*	*delfeeno*
hare	**lepre** *(f.)*	*lepreh*

hedgehog	**riccio** *(m.)*	*reecho*
mouse	**topo** *(m.)*	*topo*
rat	**ratto** *(m.)*	*rat-to*
seal (Mediterranean monk ~)	**foca** *(f.)* **monaca**	*foka monaka*
wolf	**lupo** *(m.)*	*loopo*

Birds

blackbird	**merlo** *(m.)*	*mayrlo*
blackcap (warbler)	**capinera** *(f.)*	*kapeenayra*
cormorant	**cormorano** *(m.)*	*kormorano*
crow	**corvo** *(m.)*	*korvo*
dove	**colomba** *(f.)*	*kolomba*
duck	**anatra** *(f.)*	*anatra*
falcon	**falco** *(m.)*	*falko*
flamingo	**fenicottero** *(m.)*	*fayneekot-tayro*
nightingale	**usignolo** *(m.)*	*oozeenyolo*
partridge	**pernice** *(f.)*	*payrneecheh*
pelican	**pellicano** *(m.)*	*payl-leekano*
pigeon	**piccione** *(m.)*	*peechoneh*
robin redbreast	**pettirosso** *(m.)*	*payt-teerosso*
seagull	**gabbiano** *(m.)*	*gab-byano*
sparrow	**passero** *(m.)*	*passayro*
swallow / swift	**rondine** *(f.)*	*rondeeneh*
vulture	**avvoltoio** *(m.)*	*av-voltoyo*

Insects & spiders

ant	**formica** *(f.)*	*formeeka*
bee	**ape** *(f.)*	*apeh*
spider	**ragno** *(m.)*	*ranyo*
wasp	**vespa** *(m.)*	*vespa*

Reptiles

grass snake	biscia (f.)	beesha
lizard	lucertola (f.)	loochayrtola
snake	serpente (m.)	sayrpenteh
turtle	tartaruga (f.)	tartarooga
viper	vipera (f.)	veepayra

Fish & shellfish

anchovy	acciuga (f.)	achooga
crab	granchio (m.)	grankyo
eel	anguilla (f.)	angweel-la
grouper (white ~)	cernia (f.) bianca	chayrnya byanka
mackerel	sgombro (m.)	zgombro
mullet (red ~)	triglia (f.)	treelya
octopus	polpo (m.)	polpo
sea bass	spigola (m.)	speegola
sea bream (bogue ~)	boga (f.)	boga
sea bream (gilthead ~)	orata (f.)	orata
sea bream (porgy)	pagro (m.)	pagro
sea bream (red ~)	pagello (m.)	pajel-lo
sea bream (saddled ~)	occhiata (f.)	ok-kyata
sea bream (Salema porgy ~)	salpa (f.)	salpa
sea bream (white ~)	sarago (m.) maggiore	sarago maj-joreh
sea urchin	riccio (m.) di mare	reecho dee mareh
shrimp / prawn	gamberetto (m.)	gambayret-to
shrimp / prawn (king ~)	gambero (m.)	gambayro
snapper (red ~)	dentice (m.)	daynteechee
squid	calamaro (m.)	kalamaro
swordfish	pesce (m.) spada	paysheh spada
tuna	tonno (m.)	ton-no
whitebait	bianchetti / gianchetti (m.)	byanket-tee / janket-tee

⤴ Accommodation

There are a range of places to stay to suit all tastes:

I'm looking for a ...	Sto cercando un / uno / una / un'...	sto chaykando oon / oono / oona / oon
bed & breakfast.	camera (f.) B&B.	kamayra bee-and-bee
cabin.	bungalow. (m.)	boongalo
campsite.	campeggio. (m.)	kampej-jo
farm holiday.	agriturismo. (m.)	agreetooreezmo
furnished apartment.	appartamento (m.) ammobiliato.	ap-partamento am-mobeelyato
guest house.	pensione. (f.)	paynsyoneh
hotel.	albergo. (m.)	albayrgo
youth hostel.	ostello (m.) della gioventù.	ostel-lo del-la jovayntoo

Making a reservation

If you call in advance, add **prenotare** *to reserve* to the below: **Vorrei prenotare...** To ask for *twin beds* it's **letti separati**.

I would like ...	Vorrei...	vorrey
a single room.	una camera singola.	oona kamayra seengola
two single rooms.	due camere singole.	dooeh kamayreh seengoleh
a double room.	una camera doppia.	oona kamayra dop-pya
a double room with a double bed.	una camera con letto matrimoniale.	oona kamayra kon let-to matreemonyaleh

We'll stay for ...	Rimarremo per...	reemarremo payr
two nights.	due notti.	dooeh not-tee
one week.	una settimana.	oona sayt-teemana

Is breakfast included?
È compresa la prima colazione?
eh kompr**ay**za la pr**ee**ma kolats**yo**neh

How much is one night with breakfast?
Quanto costa una notte con la colazione?
k**wa**nto k**o**sta **oo**na n**o**t-teh kon la kolats**yo**neh

Some hotels offer **mezza pensione** *half-board*, which means two meals are included in the price: breakfast and dinner.

At the hotel

I've reserved a room in the name of …
Ho prenotato una camera a nome di…
o praynot**a**to **oo**na kam**a**yra a n**o**meh dee

We would like a room with a sea view, if possible.
Vorremmo una camera con vista mare, se è possibile.
vorr**ay**m-mo **oo**na kam**a**yra kon v**ee**sta m**a**reh say eh poss**ee**beeleh

I would like a quiet room with a balcony.
Vorrei una camera tranquilla con balcone.
vorr**ey oo**na kam**a**yra trankw**ee**l-la kon balk**o**neh

Is there air conditioning?
C'è l'aria condizionata?
che l**a**rya kondeetsyon**a**ta

Can you call a taxi for me, please?
Mi chiama un taxi, per favore?
mee k**ya**ma oon t**a**ksee payr fav**o**reh

Checking out

Could I have the bill, please?
Mi prepara il conto, per favore.
mee praypara eel konto payr favoreh

Breakfast and services

Breakfast

Although it can vary from region to region as well as from home to home, a typical Italian breakfast (**la colazione**) almost invariably includes an **espresso**, **cappuccino** or **caffè latte** accompanied by something sweet – pastries or baked goods. See 'Other beverages' for more on the types of coffee.

Can I have ...?
Posso avere...?
posso avayreh

Where is/are ...?
Dov'è / dove sono...?
doveh / doveh sono

butter	**burro** *(m.)*	*boorro*
cereal	**cereali** *(m.)*	*chayrayalee*
coffee	**caffè** *(m.)*	*kaf-feh*
eggs (scrambled / boiled / with bacon)	**uova** *(m.)* **(strapazzate / sode / con pancetta)**	*wova (strapat-tsateh / sodeh / kon panchet-ta)*
fruit juice	**succo** *(m.)* **di frutta**	*sook-ko dee froot-ta*
honey	**miele** *(m.)*	*myayleh*
hot chocolate	**cioccolata** *(f.)*	*chok-kolata*
milk	**latte** *(m.)*	*lat-teh*
omelette	**frittata** *(f.)*	*freet-tata*
sausages	**salsiccia** *(f.)*	*salseecha*
sugar	**zucchero** *(m.)*	*dsook-kero*
tea	**tè** *(m.)*	*teh*

Services

airport shuttle	navetta (f.) aeroportuale	navet-ta a-ayroportwaleh
babysitting	babysitting	baybeeseet-teeng
bar	bar (m.)	bar
business center	business center (m.)	beeznays sentayr
car rental	noleggio (m.) auto	nolayj-jo aoto
disabled access	strutture (f. pl.) accessibili a ospiti disabili	stroot-tooreh achesseebeelee a ospeetee deezabeelee
dry cleaning	lavaggio (m.) a secco	lavaj-jo sek-ko
family room	camera (f.) per famiglie	kamayra payr fameelyeh
garden	giardino (m.)	jardeeno
hairdryer	phon (m.) / asciugacapelli (m.)	fon / ashoogakapel-lee
internet	Internet (f.)	eentayrnayt
internet connection	connessione (f.) Internet	kon-nayss-yoneh eentayrnayt
ironing	stiro (m.)	steero
laundrette / laundromat	lavanderia (f.)	lavandayreea
left-luggage storage	deposito (m.) bagagli	daypozeeto bagalyee
meeting room	sala (f.) riunioni	sala ree-oonyonee
newspapers	giornali (m.)	jornalee
non-smoking room(s)	camera/-e (f.) non-fumatori	kamayra/-eh nonfoomatoree
parking	parcheggio (m.)	parkej-jo
pets allowed	animali ammessi	aneemalee am-messee
private beach	spiaggia (f.) privata	spyaj-ja preevata
reception	reception (m.)	raysepshun
restaurant	ristorante (m.)	reestoranteh
room service	servizio (m.) in camera	sayrveetsyo een kamayra
smoking area	area (f.) fumatori	araya foomatoree

swimming pool	**piscina** (f.)	peesh**ee**na
television (satellite ~)	**televisione** (f.) **via satellite**	taylayvee**zy**oneh v**ee**a sat**ay**l-leeteh
terrace	**terrazza** (f.)	tayr**ra**t-tsa

Resolving issues

In case you have any problems during your stay:

Excuse me ...	Scusi...	sk**oo**zee
the fan	**il ventilatore**	eel vaynteelat**o**reh
the faucet/tap	**il rubinetto**	eel roobeen**e**t-to
the heating	**il riscaldamento**	eel reeskaldam**e**nto
the lamp	**la lampada**	la l**a**mpada
the light	**la luce**	la l**oo**cheh
the lightbulb	**la lampadina**	la lampad**ee**na
the socket / the plug	**la presa di corrente / la spina**	la pr**ay**za dee korr**e**nteh / la sp**ee**na
the switch	**l'interruttore**	leentayrroot-t**o**reh
the ventilation system	**il sistema di ventilazione**	eel seest**e**ma dee vaynteelats**y**oneh

... doesn't work.
... non funziona.
non foonts**yo**na

... is broken.
... è rotto/-a.
eh r**o**t-to/-a

The sink is blocked.
Il lavandino è intasato.
eel lavand**ee**no eh eentaz**a**to

There's no (hot) water.
Non c'è acqua (calda).
non che **a**kwa (k**a**lda)

Here are some other terms that might come in handy: **la chiave** *the key*, **un bagno privato** *ensuite bathroom*, **un asciugamano** *a towel*, **la carta igienica** *toilet paper* or **rumoroso** *noisy*.

↗ Eating and drinking

Italian food is world-famous and is very often good wherever you choose to eat. There are a range of options for eating out:
- **mensa** *[mensa]*: cafeteria or dining hall
- **osteria** *[ostayreea]*: restaurant with simple, regional food
- **pizzeria** *[peet-tsayreea]*: often with a wood-fired pizza oven
- **ristorante** *[reestoranteh]*: restaurant with more upscale cuisine
- **tavola calda** *[tavola kalda]*: snack bar with pre-made dishes
- **trattoria** *[trat-toreea]*: family-run restaurant with local dishes

Il pranzo *lunch* and **la cena** *dinner* can consist of several courses: **un antipasto** *appetizer*, **il primo** *starter*, **il secondo** *main course*, with **un contorno** *side dish*, followed by **il formaggio** *cheese* and/or **il dolce** *dessert*. Some restaurants have a **menù**, a fixed-price set of courses.

Note that a service charge is almost always automatically included – the menu should indicate if it is factored into the prices (**servizio incluso**) or added separately to the bill. As a result, tipping is not common, although you might leave 2 or 3 euros as a token of appreciation. Sometimes the menu will also indicate a **coperto** *cover charge*, which might include bread.

At the restaurant

I would like to reserve a table for four for 9 p.m.
Vorrei prenotare un tavolo per quattro per le 9.
vorrey praynotareh oon tavolo payr kwat-tro payr lay noveh

My name is ... I reserved a table for four.
Mi chiamo... ho prenotato un tavolo per quattro.
mee kyamo... o praynotato oon tavolo payr kwat-tro

We don't have a reservation.
Non abbiamo prenotato.
non ab-byamo praynotato

Good evening. A table for three, please.
Buonasera. Un tavolo per tre, per cortesia.
bwonasayra oon tavolo payr treh payr kortayzeea

Once you're seated, you may have some questions:

Could we have a menu, please?
Vorremmo il menù, per favore.
vorraym-mo eel maynoo payr favoreh

What do you recommend today?
Cosa ci consiglia oggi?
koza chee konseelya oj-jee

Do you have vegetarian dishes?
Avete piatti vegetariani?
avayteh pyat-tee vayjaytaryanee

We would like (some) ...	Vorremmo (del / dello / della / dell' / dei / degli / delle)	vorraym-mo (del / del-lo/-a / del / day / delyee / del-leh)
appetizers/starters.	**antipasti.** (m.)	anteepastee
bread.	**pane.** (m.)	paneh
cake. / dessert.	**torta.** (f.) / **dolce.** (m.)	torta / dolcheh
cheese.	**formaggio.** (m.)	formaj-jo
chips/fries.	**patate** (f.) **fritte.**	patateh freet-teh
fish.	**pesce.** (m.)	paysheh
fruit.	**frutta.** (f.)	froot-ta
game. (wild ~)	**selvaggina.** (f.)	selvaj-jeena

ice cream.	**gelato.** *(m.)*	*jay*lato
meat.	**carne.** *(f.)*	*kar*neh
mustard.	**senape.** *(f.)*	*say*napeh
olive oil.	**olio** *(m.)* **d'oliva.**	*o*lyo do*lee*va
pasta.	**pastasciutta.** *(f.)*	pastash*oo*t-ta
pepper.	**pepe.** *(m.)*	*pe*peh
rice.	**riso.** *(m.)*	*ree*zo
salt.	**sale.** *(m.)*	*sa*leh
seafood.	**frutti** *(m.)* **di mare.**	fr*oo*tee dee *ma*reh
soup.	**minestra.** *(f.)*	mee*nes*tra
sugar.	**zucchero.** *(m.)*	ts*oo*k-*kay*ro
sweets/pastries.	**dolci.** *(m.)*	*dol*chee
vegetables.	**verdure.** *(f.)*	vayrd*oo*reh
vinegar.	**aceto.** *(m.)*	a*chay*to
water. (mineral ~)	**acqua** *(f.)* **(minerale).**	*a*kwa (meenay*ra*leh)

For a quick, light bite (**uno spuntino**) or an afternoon snack (**una merenda**), you might want:

hamburger	**hamburger** *(m.)*	am*boor*gayr
hot drinks / herbal teas	**bevande** *(f.)* **calde / infusi** *(m.)*	ba*van*deh *kal*deh / een*foo*zee
ice creams	**gelati** *(m.)*	*jay*latee
salads	**insalate** *(f.)*	een*sa*lateh
sandwich	**panino** *(m.)*	pa*nee*no
savoury crêpes (buckwheat)	**galette** *(f.)* **salate (al grano saraceno)**	ga*layt*-teh *sa*lateh (al *gra*no sara*chay*no)
sweet crêpes	**crêpes** *(f.)* **dolci**	krep *dol*chee
toasted sandwich	**toast** *(m.)*	tost
waffles	**cialde** *(f.)*	*chal*deh

To indicate something on display:

Please give me ...	Per favore, mi dia...	payr favoreh mee deea
a piece of this.	una porzione di questo.	oona portsyoneh dee kwaysto
one of these and two of those.	uno di questi, due di quelli.	oono dee kwaystee dooeh dee kwayl-lee
on the left / on the right	a sinistra / a destra	a seeneestra / a destra
at the top / on the bottom	di sopra / di sotto	dee sopra / dee sot-to

Or if you're missing some cutlery:

Can you bring me another ...
Mi porta un altro / un'altra...
mee porta oon altro / oonaltra

cup	**tazza** *(f.)*	*tat-tsa*
fork	**forchetta** *(f.)*	*forket-ta*
glass	**bicchiere** *(m.)*	*beek-kyayreh*
knife	**coltello** *(m.)*	*koltel-lo*
plate	**piatto** *(m.)*	*pyat-to*
spoon	**cucchiaio** *(m.)*	*kook-kylo*

Enjoy your meal!
Buon appetito!
bwon ap-payteeto

Cheers!
Salute! / Cin cin!
salooteh / cheen cheen

Asking for the bill

The bill/check, please.
Il conto, per favore.
eel konto payr favoreh

Can I pay with a credit card?
Posso pagare con la carta di credito?
posso pagareh kon la karta dee kredeeto

I didn't order this.
Non ho ordinato questo.
non o ordeenato kwaysto

Specialities and traditional dishes

Italian cuisine is very diverse from region to region. Here are some specialities you may come across.

Starters, appetizers & soups

- **acquacotta** *[akwakot-ta]*: vegetable soup made with tomatoes, peppers, celery, eggs, artichokes or mushrooms
- **antipasti misti** *[anteepastee meeslee]*: assorted appetizers (raw or marinated vegetables, deli meats, cheese, etc.)
- **bruschetta** *[broosket-ta]*: grilled bread spread with tomato, olive oil, garlic and salt or other toppings
- **caponata palermitana** *[kaponata palermeetana]*: a Sicilian dish based on cooked aubergine (eggplant) and capers
- **cazzimperio** *[kat-tseempayryo]*: sliced raw vegetables with an olive-oil based sauce for dipping
- **mesciua** *[meshooa]*: Ligurian soup made with buckwheat, beans and chickpeas
- **millecosedde** *[mil-laykossayd-deh]*: thick soup from Calabria with vegetables, pulses (peas, beans, etc.) and pasta
- **minestrone** *[meenestroneh]*: vegetable soup (ingredients vary)
- **pancotto** *[pankot-to]*: bread soup with added ingredients such as cheese, eggs and fresh tomatoes
- **paparot** *[paparot]*: spinach and polenta soup from Friuli

- **ribollita** [reebol-leeta]: (literally, 'reboiled') a hearty Tuscan stew with bread, beans and vegetables
- **sopa coada** [sopa kwada]: Venetian pigeon soup with bread, meat and cheese
- **stracciatella** [strachatel-la]: Roman-style egg drop soup

Cold cuts, meat- & egg-based dishes

- **abbacchio** [ab-bak-kyo]: suckling lamb
- **abbacchio a scottadito** [ab-bak-kyo a skot-tadeeto]: pan-fried lamb chops
- **animelle** [aneemayl-leh]: sweetbreads (thymus or pancreas)
- **arancini** [arancheenee]: fried rice balls coated in breadcrumbs
- **batsoà** [batsoa]: pig's feet, deboned, breaded and fried
- **braciolone (napoletano)** [bracholoneh napolaytano]: rolled beef stuffed with provolone cheese and ham
- **bresaola** [brezaola]: salted, air-cured, aged beef
- **burtleina** [boortleyna]: a thin, crispy crêpe made with lard
- **carbonada** [karbonada]: beef stew served with polenta
- **carne trita(ta)** [karneh treeta(ta)]: minced/ground beef
- **carpaccio** [karpacho]: thin slices of raw meat
- **coietas** [koyaytas]: rolled, stuffed beef
- **cotechinata** [kotaykeenata]: rolled pork rind stuffed with garlic, parsley and bacon and cooked in tomato sauce
- **cutturiddi** [koot-tooreed-dee]: lamb stew with tomatoes, onions and celery
- **favata** [favata]: bean stew with sausage, tomatoes and herbs
- **finanziera** [feenantsyayra]: sweetbreads, offal and mushrooms
- **fregnacce** [frenyacheh]: pockets of pasta stuffed with meat, sausage and vegetables
- **jota** [yota]: bean soup with cabbage, potatoes and smoked pork rind
- **mozzetta** [mod-dset-ta]: salted and cured mountain goat

- **ossobuco** [ossobooko]: braised veal shanks with broth
- **piccata** [peek-kata] : veal with a lemon and white wine sauce
- **polpette** [polpayt-teh]: meatballs
- **porchetta** [porket-ta]: boneless pork roast
- **sanguinaccio** [sangweenacho]: black pudding (blood sausage)
- **scottiglia** [skot-teelya]: rich meat and tomato stew
- **stracotto** [strakot-to]: Italian pot roast
- **stufatino** [stoofateeno]: beef stew with tomatoes and herbs
- **torcinelli** [torcheenel-lee]: stew with lamb tripe and sweetbreads
- **zampetto / zampone** [dsampet-to / dsamponeh]: pork knuckle

Seafood dishes

- **acquapazza** [akwapat-tsa]: poached white fish or fish broth
- **baccalà** [bak-kala]: dried and salted cod
- **bianchetti** [byanket-tee]: fried whitebait (small fish eaten whole)
- **cassola** [kassola]: fish soup from Sardinia
- **impepata di cozze** [eempepata dee kot-tseh]: peppered mussels
- **scampi** [skampee]: prawns with butter, garlic and white wine
- **stoccafisso** [stok-kafeesso]: stockfish (unsalted air-dried cod)

Pasta & pizzas

Certain of these are well-known outside Italy – **ravioli** [ravyolee], **maccheroni** [mak-kayronee], **spaghetti** [spagayt-tee] and **penne** [payn-neh] – but here are some less common types you could try:
- **agnolini / agnolotti** [anyoleenee / anyolot-tee]: round ravioli
- **bucatini** [bookateenee]: thick spaghetti with a hole in the centre
- **caciuni** [kachoonee]: sweet dessert ravioli
- **canneroni** [kan-nayronee]: short pasta tubes
- **capelli d'angelo** [kapel-lee danjaylo]: ('angel hair') very thin pasta
- **cappelletti / cappellacci** [kap-pel-let-tee / kap-pel-lachee]: ('little hats') small meat-filled pasta

- **casoncelli** [kazonchel-lee]: butterfly-shaped ravioli
- **cavatelli** [kavatel-lee]: pasta that looks like little hot dog buns
- **conchiglie** [konkeelyeh]: pasta shells
- **culurgione** [kooloorjoneh]: stuffed pasta pockets from Sardinia
- **focaccia** [fokacha]: flat bread with olive oil and herbs
- **fregola** [fraygola]: small couscous-like pasta balls from Sardinia
- **garganelli** [garganel-lee]: ridged pasta quills
- **gnocchi** [nyok-kee]: dumplings made from flour and potatoes
- **laganelle** [laganel-leh]: long, flat pasta ribbons
- **maltagliati** [maltalyatee]: irregularly cut pasta scraps
- **marille** [mareel-leh]: scroll-like pasta designed to hold sauce
- **marubini** [maroobeenee]: pasta stuffed with meat, bread, parmesan, courgette (**zucchini**) and egg
- **orecchiette** [orek-kyayt-teh]: ('little ears') homemade dented disc-shaped pasta served with rapini or tomato sauce
- **paniscia novarese** [paneesha novarayzeh]: a sort of risotto with rice, beans, onions, cabbage and salami
- **panzerotti** [pandserot-tee]: savoury or sweet calzones
- **pappardelle** [pap-pardel-leh]: broad, flat pasta ribbons
- **pasta filante** [pasta feelanteh]: pasta with melted cheese
- **pettole** [pet-toleh]: pasta squares (or fried dough balls)
- **piccagge** [peek-kaj-jeh]: long pasta ribbons served with pesto or artichoke and mushroom sauce
- **pici** [peechee]: thick, hand-rolled spaghetti-like pasta
- **pizzoccheri** [peet-tsok-kayree]: short flat pasta ribbons made from buckwheat and served with cabbage and potatoes
- **rotolo** [rotolo]: a sheet of pasta spread with a filling (e.g. spinach, ricotta or meat), rolled up and then sliced and cooked
- **sardenaria** [sardenarya]: a pizza from San Remo topped with a tomato sauce, olives, capers and sardines
- **stringozzi** [streengot-tsee]: fresh shoelace-like wheat pasta
- **tubetti** [toobet-tee]: short pasta tubes

- **vincisgrassi** *[veencheesgrassee]*: baked lasagne
- **ziti** *[dseetee]*: smooth pasta tubes

Vegetable dishes
- **caponet** *[kaponet]*: stuffed cabbage
- **ciammotta / cianfotta** *[cham-mot-ta / chanfot-ta]*: a dish similar to ratatouille (peppers, aubergines, tomatoes, etc.)
- **ciaudedda** *[chaodayd-da]*: vegetable stew with artichokes, onions, potatoes, beans and bacon
- **cibuddau** *[cheebood-dao]*: onion-based dish from Sardinia
- **ciceri e tria** *[cheecheree ay treea]*: chickpeas and pasta
- **crocchette** *[krok-kayt-teh]*: potato croquettes
- **erbazzone** *[ayrbat-tsoneh]*: spinach pie
- **fiori di zucca** *[fyoree dee dsook-ka]*: stuffed and fried squash (**zucchini**) blossoms
- **impanada** *[eempanada]*: vegetable, meat or fish pie
- **infarinata** *[eenfareenata]*: Tuscan bean, polenta and vegetable soup, often containing bacon or lard
- **malfatti** *[malfat-tee]*: ricotta and spinach dumplings
- **mesta e fasoi** *[mesta ay fazoy]*: polenta cooked with beans
- **peperonata** *[paypayronata]*: stewed peppers, onions and tomatoes

Sweets & pastries
- **amaretti** *[amarayt-tee]*: almond macaroons
- **bisciola** *[beeshola]*: fruit and nut bread
- **bonet** *[bonet]*: cake made with chocolate, rum and macaroons
- **bostrengo** *[bostrayngo]*: cake made with rice, chocolate, dried fruit and nuts
- **brut e bon (brutti ma buoni)** *[brootaybon (broot-tee ma bwonee)]*: almond or hazelnut meringue cookies
- **budino** *[boodeeno]*: creamy custard pudding
- **bussolà** *[boossola]*: lemony butter biscuits or cake

- **cannoli** [kan-nolee]: tube-shaped pastries with a creamy filling
- **cantucci / cantuccini** [kantoochee / kantoocheenee]: also known as **biscotti**, these crunchy twice-baked cookies can be dipped in dessert wine (**vin santo**)
- **cassata alla siciliana** [kassata al-la seecheelyana]: sponge cake layered with chocolate, ricotta cheese and candied fruit
- **cavallucci** [kaval-loochee]: Tuscan anise-seed biscuits with hazelnuts, candied fruits and spices
- **chinulille** [keenooleel-leh]: pastries stuffed with cinnamon-flavoured ricotta and bits of candied lemon
- **colomba** [kolomba]: ('dove') a traditional Easter cake similar to a **panettone**, made from sweet brioche with candied fruit
- **cornetto** [kornayt-to]: croissant (often filled)
- **crostoli / galani** [krostolee / galanee]: sweet fritters
- **fiadoni alla trentina** [fyadonee al-la traynteena]: pastries stuffed with a filling of almonds, honey, cinnamon and rum
- **offelle** [of-fel-leh]: oval-shaped shortbread biscuits
- **Ossi da Morto** [ossee da morto]: ('bones of the dead') very crunchy almond and hazelnut biscuits
- **panelle** [panel-leh]: savoury fritters made from chickpea flour
- **panforte** [panforteh]: a chewy, candy-like fruitcake made from almonds, honey, candied fruits and spices
- **papassinas** [papasseenas]: diamond-shaped almond cookies
- **pastini di mandorle** [pasteenee dee mandorleh]: almond and apricot cookies
- **ricciarelli** [reecharel-lee]: Tuscan almond biscuits
- **sebadas** [sebadas]: round fried cheese and honey pastries
- **tiramisù** [teerameesoo]: sponge fingers soaked in strong coffee and layered with mascarpone and cream mixed with Marsala wine, then sprinkled with cocoa powder

Food vocabulary

Here is some vocabulary that might be useful when eating out or shopping. Organic food is labelled **biologico**.

Meat and poultry

Meat **la carne**, *poultry* **il pollame**, *cold cuts* **i salumi**

beef	**manzo** *(m.)*	mandso
breast	**petto** *(m.)*	pet-to
brochette / skewer	**spiedino / spiedo** *(m.)*	sp**yay**deeno / sp**yay**do
chicken	**pollo** *(m.)*	pol-lo
chop	**braciola** *(f.)*	br**a**chola
cold cuts	**salumi** *(m.)*	sal**oo**mee
duck	**anatra** *(f.)*	**a**natra
eggs	**uova** *(m.)*	**wo**va
game (wild ~)	**selvaggina** *(f.)*	selvaj-j**ee**na
goose	**oca** *(f.)*	**o**ka
ham	**prosciutto** *(m.)*	prosh**oo**t-to
hare	**lepre** *(f.)*	lepreh
hen	**gallina** *(f.)*	gal-l**ee**na
horse / pig meat	**carne** *(f.)* **equina / suina**	karneh ek**wee**na / sw**ee**na
kid (goat)	**capretto** *(m.)*	kapr**ay**t-to
kidneys	**rognoncini** *(m.)*	ronyonch**ee**nee
lamb	**agnello** *(m.)*	any**ay**l-lo
lamb skewers	**arrosticini** *(m.)*	arrosteech**ee**nee
leg / thigh	**coscia** *(f.)*	k**o**sha
liver	**fegato** *(m.)*	f**ay**gato
omelette	**frittata** *(f.)*	freet-t**a**ta
pheasant	**fagiano** *(m.)*	faj**a**no
pigeon / squab	**piccione** *(m.)*	peech**o**neh

pork	**maiale** (m.)	m**ia**leh
quail	**quaglia** (f.)	kw**a**lya
rabbit	**coniglio** (m.)	kon**ee**lyo
sausages / salamis	**insaccati** (m.)	eensak-k**a**tee
shank	**stinco** (m.)	st**ee**nko
snails	**lumache** (f.)	loom**a**keh
steak	**bistecca** (f.)	bist**ayk**-ka
steak (rib-eye ~)	**costata** (f.)	kost**a**ta
tongue	**lingua** (f.)	l**ee**ngwa
tripe	**trippa** (f.)	tr**ee**p-pa
turkey	**tacchino** (m.)	tak-k**ee**no
veal	**vitello** (m.)	veet**el**-lo
venison	**cervo** (m.)	ch**ay**rvo

Fish & shellfish

Fish **il pesce**, *shellfish* **i frutti di mare**. See also the 'Fish & shellfish' section in 'Animals'.

anchovies	**acciughe** (f.)	ach**oo**gheh
clams	**vongole** (f.)	v**o**ngoleh
cod	**merluzzo** (m.)	merl**oo**t-tso
crab	**granchio** (m.)	gr**a**nkyo
cuttlefish / sepia	**seppia** (f.)	s**e**p-pya
eel	**anguilla** (f.)	angw**ee**l-la
fish	**pesce** (m.)	p**ay**sheh
fishing	**pesca** (f.)	p**e**ska
lavarets (a whitefish)	**lavarelli** (m.)	lavar**e**l-lee
lobster	**aragosta** (f.)	arag**o**sta
mullet	**cefalo** (m.)	ch**ay**falo
mussels	**cozze** (f.)	k**o**t-tseh

octopus	**polpi** *(m. pl.)*	**po**lpee
oysters	**ostriche** *(f.)*	**o**streekeh
perch	**persico** *(m.)*	**pay**rseeko
pike	**luccio** *(m.)*	**loo**cho
ray	**razza** *(f.)*	**rat**-tsa
salmon	**salmone** *(m.)*	sal**mo**neh
sardines	**sarde** *(f.)*	**sar**deh
scallops	**capesante** *(f.)*	kapay**san**teh
sea bass	**branzino** *(m.)*	brand**see**no
sea bream (gilthead ~)	**orata** *(f.)*	o**ra**ta
sea bream (white ~)	**sarago** *(m.)*	sa**ra**go
seafood	**frutti** *(m.)* **di mare**	**froot**-tee dee **ma**reh
shellfish	**crostacei** *(m.)*	kros**ta**chey
shrimp / prawn	**gambero** *(m.)*	**gam**bero
shrimps / prawns	**gamberoni** *(m.)*	gambe**ro**nee
sole	**sogliola** *(f.)*	so**lyo**la
spider crab	**granseola** *(f.)*	gran**sayo**la
squid	**calamari** *(m. pl.)*	kala**ma**ree
squilla (mantis shrimp)	**cicala** *(f.)*	chee**ka**la
trout	**trota** *(f.)*	**tro**ta
tuna	**tonno** *(m.)*	**ton**-no
turbot	**rombo** *(m.)*	**rom**bo

Vegetables

Vegetables **le verdure**

artichokes / baby artichokes	**carciofi / carciofini** *(m.)*	kar**cho**fee / karcho**fee**nee
asparagus	**asparagi** *(m. pl.)*	aspa**ra**jee
aubergines / eggplants	**melanzane** *(f.)*	meland**sa**neh
avocado	**avocado** *(m.)*	avo**ka**do

beet	**barbabietola** *(f.)*	barbab*yay*tola
broad beans	**fave** *(f.)*	*fav*eh
cabbage	**cavolo** *(m.)*	*kav*olo
cabbage (Savoy ~)	**verza** *(f.)*	v*ay*rdsa
carrot	**carota** *(f.)*	kar*o*ta
cauliflower	**cavolfiore** *(m.)*	kavolf*yo*reh
chickpeas	**ceci** *(m.)*	*chay*chee
courgettes / zucchinis	**zucchine** *(f.)* / **zucchini** *(m.)*	dsook-k*ee*neh/-ee
escarole (an endive)	**scarola** *(f.)*	skar*o*la
fennel	**finocchio** *(m.)*	feen*o*k-kyo
green beans	**fagiolini** *(m.)*	fajol*ee*nee
lentils	**lenticchie** *(m.)*	lent*ee*k-kyeh
lettuce	**lattuga** *(f.)*	lat-t*oo*ga
mushrooms	**funghi** *(m.)*	f*oo*nghee
mushrooms (chanterelle ~)	**cantarelli** *(m.)*	kantarel-lee
mushroom (field ~)	**prataiolo** *(m.)*	prat*l*olo
mushrooms (porcini ~)	**funghi** *(m.)* **porcini**	f*oo*nghee porch*ee*nee
onions / baby onions	**cipolle** / **cipolline** *(f.)*	cheep*o*l-leh / cheepol-*lee*neh
peas	**piselli** *(m.)*	peez*ay*l-lee
peppers	**peperoni** *(m.)*	paypayr*o*nee
potatoes	**patate** *(f.)*	pat*a*teh
pumpkin	**zucca** *(f.)*	ds*oo*k-ka
rocket / arugula	**ruchetta** / **rucola** *(f.)*	r*oo*ket-ta / r*oo*kola
salad	**insalata** *(f.)*	eensal*a*ta
spinach	**spinaci** *(m.)*	speen*a*chee
tomatoes / dried tomatoes	**pomodori** *(m.)* / **pomodori secchi**	pomod*o*ree / pomod*o*ree sek-kee
truffle	**tartufo** *(m.)*	tart*oo*fo
turnip	**rapa** *(f.)*	r*a*pa
vegetable / vegetables	**verdura/-e** *(f.)*	verd*oo*ra/-eh

CONVERSING

Fruits & nuts

Fruit **la frutta**, *nuts* **le noce** or **la frutta secca** (but note that there is not really a generic term for *nuts* in Italian – usually the type of nut is referred to specifically, e.g. **la noce** *walnut*.

apple	**mela** *(f.)*	**may**la
apricot	**albicocca** *(f.)*	albeek**ok**-ka
cherry	**ciliegia** *(f.)*	cheely**ayy**ja
dates	**datteri** *(m.)*	dat-tayree
fig	**fico** *(m.)*	feeko
fruit	**frutta** *(f.)*	froot-ta
grapefruit	**pompelmo** *(m.)*	pompelmo
grapes (green / red) / raisins	**uva** *(f.)* **(bianca / nera)** / **uva** *(f.)* **passa**	**oo**va (**by**anka / **nay**ra) / **oo**va passa
lemon	**limone** *(m.)*	leemoneh
orange / oranges	**arancia / arance** *(f.)*	arancha/-eh
pears	**pere** *(f.)*	payreh
plum	**prugna** *(f.)*	proony**a**
pomegranate	**melagrana** *(f.)*	maylagrana
raspberries	**lamponi** *(m.)*	lamponee
strawberries	**fragole** *(f.)*	fragoleh
walnut	**noce** *(f.)*	nocheh
watermelon	**cocomero** *(m.)* / **anguria** *(f.)*	kokomayro / ang**oo**rya

Cooking methods and sauces

Cooking methods

baked ('in the oven')	**al forno**	al forno
boiled	**lesso**	lesso
braised	**brasato**	brazato
cold	**freddo**	fred-do

fresh	fresco	fresko
fried	fritto	freet-to
grilled ('on the grill')	griglia (alla ~)	al-la greelya
raw	crudo	kroodo
roasted	arrosto	arrosto
smoked	affumicato	af-foomeekato
stuffed	ripieni	reepyaynee

To specify how you want your dish cooked:

I don't want the meat ...
La carne, non la voglio...
la karneh non la volyo

I don't want the fish ...
Il pesce, non lo voglio...
eel paysheh non lo volyo

overcooked	troppo cotto/-a	trop-po kot-to/-a
boiled	bollito/-a	bol-leeto/-a

I'd like it ...	Preferisco che sia...	prayfayreesko kay seea
very rare.	molto al sangue.	molto al sangweh
rare.	al sangue.	al sangweh
well-done.	ben cotto/-a.	ben kot-to/-a
grilled.	ai ferri.	I ferree
steamed.	cotto a vapore.	kot-to a vaporeh
tender.	morbido.	morbeedo

The term for *medium-rare* is **con cottura media**.

Sauces, seasonings and condiments

- **abruzzese** *[abroot-tsayzeh]*: hearty meat sauce
- **aglio** *[alyo]*: garlic
- **aglio e olio** *[alyo ay olyo]*: garlic and olive oil
- **amatriciana (all'~)** *[al-lamatreechana]*: tomato sauce with salt-cured pork, onion and chili flakes
- **arrabbiata (all'~)** *[al-larrab-byata]*: spicy tomato sauce with garlic and chili flakes
- **bagnetto verde** *[banyayt-to vayrdeh]*: sauce with parsley, garlic, anchovies, capers, bread, olive oil and vinegar
- **basilico** *[bazeeleeko]*: basil
- **besciamella** *[beshamel-la]*: béchamel (butter, flour and milk)
- **bolognese (alla ~)** *[al-la bolonyayzeh]*: tomato and beef sauce
- **boscaiola (alla ~)** *[al-la boskayola]*: sauce made with mushrooms and other ingredients
- **brodo (in ~)** *[een brodo]*: in broth
- **cacciatora (alla ~)** *[al-la kachatora]*: ('hunter style') meat (often chicken) cooked in a wine and tomato sauce with herbs
- **cannella** *[kan-nel-la]*: cinnamon
- **capperi** *[kap-payree]*: capers
- **caprese** *[kaprayzeh]*: with mozzarella, tomatoes and basil
- **cartoccio** *[kartocho]*: cooking method in which the food is cooked in wax paper or aluminium foil
- **casalinga (alla ~)** *[al-la kazaleenga]*: home cooking
- **cognà** *[konya]*: a sort of chutney made with grapes, apples and other fruit, eaten with cheeses, on bread or with polenta
- **condimento** *[kondeemento]*: condiment or seasoning
- **cren** *[kren]*: horseradish
- **diavola (alla ~)** *[al-la dyavola]*: hot, spicy
- **diavolicchio** *[dyavoleek-kyo]*: 'little devil' red chili peppers
- **erbe** *[ayrbeh]*: herbs
- **fiorentina (alla ~)** *[al-la fyoraynteena]*: with spinach

- **funghi (ai ~)** *[I foonghee]*: with mushrooms
- **genovese (alla ~)** *[al-la jaynovayzeh]*: see **pesto**
- **mantecato** *[mantaykato]*: creamy or buttery
- **marinara (alla ~)** *[al-la mareenara]*: with seafood
- **milanese (alla ~)** *[al-la meelanayzeh]*: breaded veal or chicken cutlets fried in butter
- **misto/-a** *[meesto/-a]*: mixed
- **napoletana (alla ~)** *[al-la napolaytana]*: tomato and garlic sauce
- **nero (al ~)** *[al nayro]*: with cuttlefish ink
- **noce moscata** *[nocheh moskata]*: nutmeg
- **olio (d'oliva)** *[olyo doleeva]*: olive oil
- **pepe** *[paypeh]*: pepper
- **peperoncini** *[paypayroncheenee]*: chili peppers
- **pesto** *[paysto]*: sauce with fresh basil, pine nuts, olive oil, garlic, cheese (often parmesan) and salt
- **piemontese (alla ~)** *[al-la pyaymontayzeh]*: wine and truffle sauce
- **pinoli** *[peenolee]*: pine nuts
- **pizzaiola (alla ~)** *[al-la peet-tsayola]*: tomato and oregano sauce
- **pomodoro (al ~)** *[al pomodoro]*: tomato sauce
- **rafano** *[rafano]*: horseradish
- **romana (alla ~)** *[al-la romana]*: literally 'Roman-style', this can refer to several recipes with varying ingredients
- **salsa** *[salsa]*: sauce
- **saor (in ~)** *[een saor]*: sweet-and-sour sauce
- **sbirraglia (alla ~)** *[al-la zbeerralya]*: with white chicken meat
- **scabeccio / scapece (in ~)** *[een skabaycho / skapaycheh]*: marinated in oil and vinegar before cooking ('escabeche')
- **senape** *[saynapeh]*: mustard
- **siciliana (alla ~)** *[al-la seecheelyana]*: sauce with aubergines, anchovies, olives, capers, garlic and tomatoes
- **sott'aceti** *[sot-tachaytee]*: pickled vegetables
- **sott'olio** *[sot-tolyo]*: vegetables preserved in oil
- **spezie** *[spetsyeh]*: spices

- **tocco di carne** [tok-ko dee karneh]: thick tomato and meat sauce
- **tonnato** [ton-nato]: a creamy sauce made with tuna, egg yolks, capers, anchovies and lemon juice
- **trevisana (alla ~)** [al-la trayveezana]: with radicchio
- **valdostana (alla ~)** [al-la valdostana]: breaded cutlets sautéed in wine sauce and topped with prosciutto and melted fontina cheese
- **zenzero** [dsayndsayro]: ginger

Cheeses

Everyone is familiar with parmesan and mozzarella, but in fact Italy produces many different types of cheese: soft cheeses, hard cheeses, blue cheese, **formaggio di vacca** [formaj-jo dee vak-ka] *cheese made from cow's milk*, **di capra** [dee kapra] *goat's milk* or **di pecora** [dee pekora] *sheep's milk*. Here is a selection of some you might want to try:

- **Asiago** [azyago]: a hard cow's milk cheese
- **Bel Paese** [bayl paayzeh]: a mild semi-soft cheese
- **Bitto** [beet-to]: a mainly cow's milk cheese from Lombardy
- **Bocconcini** [bok-koncheenee]: egg-sized mozzarella balls
- **Bra** [bra]: a hard, semi-aged cheese from the town of Bra
- **Branzi** [brandsee]: a semi-firm alpine cow's milk cheese
- **Bross (bruss)** [bross (brooss)]: spreadable sheep's or goat's milk cheese mixed with grappa and cream
- **Caciocavallo** [kachokaval-lo]: a teardrop-shaped cheese hung from a string that tastes similar to provolone
- **Caciotta** [kachot-ta]: a range of simple, rural cheeses
- **Caprino** [kapreeno]: soft goat's milk cheese
- **Castelmagno** [kastelmanyo]: a crumbly semi-hard cow's milk cheese that sometimes has blue veins
- **Crescenza** [kreshentsa]: a very young, mild cheese

- **Dolcelatte** *[dolchaylat-teh]*: a soft blue cheese
- **Fior di latte** *[fyor dee lat-teh]*: cow's milk mozzarella with a very mild, creamy flavour
- **Fonduta** *[fondoota]*: a fondue made from Fontina cheese
- **Fontina** *[fonteena]*: an alpine cow's milk cheese
- **Gorgonzola** *[gorgondsola]*: a buttery, crumbly blue cheese
- **Grana Padana** *[grana padana]*: a hard cheese similar to Parmesan, but slightly milder and less crumbly
- **Manteca** *[mantayka]*: balls of mozzarella-type cheese with a lump of butter inside
- **Mascarpone** *[maskarponeh]*: a very creamy soft cheese
- **Montasio** *[montazyo]*: a mild, nutty cheese
- **Mozzarella di bufala** *[mot-tsarel-la dee boofala]*: a soft, mild cheese made from the milk of domestic Italian water buffalo
- **Nostrano** *[nostrano]*: a nutty alpine cheese
- **Parmigiano-Reggiano** *[parmeejano rej-jano]*: authentic Parmesan produced in Parma and the neighbouring provinces
- **Pecorino Romano** *[paykoreeno romano]*: a hard, salty cheese made from goat's milk, often used for grated toppings
- **Provola** *[provola]* or **Provolone** *[provoloneh]*: a mellow, semi-soft cow's milk cheese that is sometimes smoked
- **Quartirolo** *[kwarteerolo]*: a soft, crumbly cow's milk cheese with a texture similar to feta
- **Ricotta** *[reekot-ta]*: creamy curds typically made from sheep's milk, with a texture similar to cottage cheese
- **Robiola** *[robyola]*: a soft, creamy cheese
- **Scamorza** *[skamordsa]*: a pear-shaped cheese similar to mozzarella but slightly more flavourful; it is often smoked
- **Stracchino** *[strak-keeno]*: a soft, young cow's milk cheese
- **Taleggio** *[talayj-jo]*: a pungent but mild soft cheese
- **Tosella** *[tozayl-la]*: an unaged white cheese; often grilled or fried

Drinks

I would like a bottle of wine, please.
Vorrei una bottiglia di vino, per favore.
vorr**ey oo**na bot-t**ee**lya dee v**ee**no payr fav**o**reh

I would like ...	Vorrei...	vorr**ey**
a beer.	una birra.	**oo**na b**ee**rra
some white wine.	del vino bianco.	del v**ee**no by**a**nko
some red wine.	del vino rosso.	del v**ee**no r**o**sso
some rosé wine.	del vino rosato.	del v**ee**no roz**a**to
a 1-litre carafe.	un litro.	oon l**ee**tro
a glass.	un bicchiere.	oon beek-ky**ay**reh
a bottle.	una bottiglia.	**oo**na bot-t**ee**lya
a half-bottle.	una mezza bottiglia.	**oo**na m**ay**d-dsa bot-t**ee**lya
a small carafe.	una piccola caraffa.	**oo**na p**ee**k-kola kar**a**f-fa

Other beverages

I would like ...	Vorrei...	vorr**ey**
a mineral water.	un'acqua minerale.	oon**a**kwa meenayr**a**leh
a sparkling mineral water.	un'acqua minerale frizzante.	oon**a**kwa meenayr**a**leh freed-ds**a**nteh
a still mineral water.	un'acqua minerale naturale.	oon**a**kwa meenayr**a**leh natoor**a**leh
a little milk.	un po' di latte.	oon po dee l**a**t-teh
a lemon soda.	una limonata.	**oo**na leemon**a**ta
an orange soda.	un'aranciata.	oonaranch**a**ta
a/an ... juice.	un succo...	oon s**oo**k-ko...
... lemon ...	di limone.	dee leem**o**neh
... orange	d'arancia.	dar**a**ncha

... pineapple ...	**di ananas.**	dee **a**nanas
... tomato ...	**di pomodoro.**	dee pomod**o**ro

The famous coffee ...

espresso with less water / with more water	**caffè** *(m.)* **ristretto / lungo**	kaf-**feh** reestr**ay**t-to / l**oo**ngo
espresso	**espresso** *(m.)*	aysp**re**sso
double espresso	**caffè** *(m.)* **doppio**	kaf-**feh** d**o**p-pyo
espresso + dash of milk	**caffè** *(m.)* **macchiato**	kaf-**feh** mak-k**ya**to
cappuccino	**cappuccino** *(m.)*	kap-poch**ee**no
decaf espresso	**caffè** *(m.)* **decaffeinato**	kaf-**feh** daykaf-fayeen**a**to

If you want a larger coffee, you can ask for a **caffè americano**, which is an espresso with extra hot water added. A **caffè latte** is a glass of hot milk mixed with a shot of espresso. Normally Italians only drink milky coffee in the morning, so if you want one at another time of day, make sure you specify this! An iced coffee (usually sweetened with sugar) is a **caffè freddo**.

⇗ Shopping

Do you happen to have ...?
Avete per caso...?
av**ay**teh payr k**a**zo

I'd like something ...	**Vorrei qualcosa...**	vorr**ey** kwalk**o**za
more affordable.	**di più conveniente.**	dee pyoo konvayny**ay**nteh
a little bigger.	**un po' più grande.**	oon po pyoo gr**a**ndeh
a little smaller.	**un po' più piccolo.**	oon po pyoo p**ee**k-kolo

How much is this?
Quanto viene questo?
kwanto vyayneh kwaysto

I'm just looking.
Do soltanto un'occhiata.
do soltanto oonok-kyata

If you decide to buy something:

Perfect, I'll take it!
Perfetto! Lo/la prendo!
payrfet-to lo/la prendo

Do you accept credit cards?
Accetta la carta di credito?
achet-ta la karta dee kredeeto

No, thank you, that will be all.
No grazie, è tutto.
no gratsyeh eh toot-to

Shops and services

Many shops in Italy usually shut for a couple of hours around 1:00, opening again at around 3:00 p.m. They stay open until around 7:30 p.m. Most are closed on Sundays.

Where is the nearest shopping centre?
Dov'è il centro commerciale più vicino?
doveh eel chentro kom-mayrchaleh pyoo veecheeno

What time does it open?
A che ora apre?
a kay ora apreh

What time does it close?
A che ora chiude?
a kay ora kyoodeh

I'm looking for a/an ...	Sto cercando un/una...	sto chayrkando oon/oona
antique store.	negozio di antiquariato.	naygotsyo dee anteekwaryato
bakery.	panetteria.	panayt-tayreea
beauty parlor.	estetista.	aystayteesta
bookstore.	libreria.	leebrayreea
butcher shop.	macelleria.	machayl-layreea
fish shop/fishmonger.	pescheria.	payskayreea
florist.	fioraio.	fyorIo
greengrocer. (produce)	fruttivendolo.	froot-teevendolo
hairdresser (for women / for men).	parrucchiere (per signora / per uomo).	parrook-kyayreh (payr seenyora / payr womo)
jewellery store.	gioielleria.	joyayl-layreea
market.	mercato.	mayrkato
newsstand.	edicola.	aydeekola
pastry shop.	pasticceria.	pasteechayreea
police station.	commissariato (di polizia).	kom-meessaryato dee poleetseea
post office.	ufficio postale.	oof-feecho postaleh
shoe-repairer/maker.	calzolaio.	kaltsolIo
shoe store.	negozio di calzature.	naygotsyo dee kaltsatooreh
souvenir shop.	negozio di souvenir.	naygotsyo dee soovayneer
supermarket.	supermercato.	soopayrmayrkato
tobacconist.	tabaccheria.	tabak-kayreea
toy store.	negozio di giocattoli.	naygotsyo dee jokat-tolee
wine shop.	enoteca.	aynoteka

Books and maps

I would like a/an ...	Vorrei un/una...	vorrey oon / oona
city map.	mappa della città.	map-pa del-la cheet-ta
road map.	mappa stradale.	map-pa stradaleh
English–Italian dictionary.	dizionario inglese-italiano.	deetsyonaryo eenglayzeh eetalyano
Italian–English dictionary.	dizionario italiano-inglese.	deetsyonaryo eetalyano eenglayzeh
pocket dictionary.	dizionario tascabile.	deetsyonaryo taskabeeleh

I would like to buy a book by ...
Vorrei comprare un libro di...
vorrey komprareh oon leebro dee

Do you have books by this author?
Avete libri di questo autore?
avayteh leebree dee kwaysto aotoreh

Or if you want a newspaper in English: **un giornale in inglese**.

Laundry and dry cleaning

I'm looking for a laundrette/laundromat.
Cerco una lavanderia.
chayrko oona lavandayreea

Could you ...	Potrebbe...	potrayb-beh
... clean ...	... pulire...	pooleereh
... iron ...	... stirare...	steerareh
... wash ...	... lavare...	lavareh
... these clothes?	... questi abiti?	kwaystee abeetee

There are/aren't stains.
Ci sono / Non ci sono macchie.
chee sono / non chee sono mak-kyeh

When will it be ready?
Quando saranno pronti?
kwando saran-no prontee

Shopping for clothes

Unfortunately, international sizes vary! Some tags label the equivalent international clothes size (**la taglia**). If you're looking for a particular colour: **azzurro** *light blue*, **blu** *dark blue*, **verde** *green*, **rosso** *red*, **rosa** *pink*, **viola** *purple*, **giallo** *yellow*, **marrone** *brown*, **grigio** *grey*, **nero** *black*, **bianco** *white*.

I would like something like this, please.
Mi piacerebbe qualcosa di simile a questo, per favore.
mee pyachayreb-beh kwalkoza dee seemeeleh a kwaysto payr favoreh

I'm size 42.
Porto la 42.
porto la kwaranta dooeh

Can I try it on?
Posso provarlo?
posso provarlo

Do you have something lighter?
Avete qualcosa di più leggero?
avayteh kwalkoza dee pyoo layj-jero

It's too ...	È troppo...	eh trop-po
big.	grande.	grandeh
small.	piccolo.	peek-kolo
tight.	stretto.	strayt-to
loose-fitting.	largo.	largo

CONVERSING

Here are some clothing and accessories:

bikini	**bikini** (m.)	bee**kee**nee
cap / beret	**berretto** (m.)	bayr**ray**t-to
coat	**cappotto** (m.)	kap-**pot**-to
dress	**abito** (m.)	**a**beeto
hat	**cappello** (m.)	kap-**pel**-lo
pyjamas	**pigiama** (m.)	pee**ja**ma
shorts	**calzoncini** (m.)	kaltson**chee**nee
skirt	**gonna** (f.)	**gon**-na
socks	**calzini** (m.)	kalt**see**nee
sportswear	**abbigliamento** (m.) **sportivo**	ab-beelya**may**nto spor**tee**vo
stockings	**calze** (f.)	**kalt**seh
sweater	**maglione** (m.)	mal**yo**neh
tracksuit	**tuta** (f.) **da ginnastica**	**too**ta da jeen-**nas**teeka
trousers	**pantaloni** (m.)	panta**lo**nee

Not to forget **le scarpe** *[lay skarpeh] shoes*, which Italy is world-famous for (**il numero** *shoe size*):

I would like a pair of sandals in size 38.
Vorrei un paio di sandali, un 38.
*vorr**ey** oon p**l**o dee sanda**lee** oon traynt**ot**-to*

ankle boots	**stivaletti** (m.)	steeva**let**-tee
boots	**stivali** (m.)	steeva**lee**
flip flops	**sandali** (m.) **da spiaggia**	sanda**lee** da sp**yaj**-ja
moccasins / loafers	**mocassini** (m.)	mokas**see**nee
tennis shoes / trainers	**scarpe** (f.) **da ginnastica**	**skar**peh da jeen-**nas**teeka

Your heel broke? One of your nicest shoes lost a buckle?

I'm looking for a shoe-repairer.
Sto cercando un calzolaio.
sto chayrkando oon kaltsolIo

Can you repair these for me?
Me le può riparare?
may lay pwo reeparareh

Smoking

La tabaccheria (or **il tabaccaio**) is often identified by a blue sign with a 'T'. Tobacconists sell not only smoking-related items, but often newspapers, stamps, local bus tickets, phone cards, postcards, etc. *An ashtray* is **un portacenere**.

carton	**stecca** (f.)	*stayk-ka*
lighter	**accendino** (m.)	*achayndeeno*

I would like a pack of ...
Vorrei un pacchetto di...
vorrey oon pak-kayt-to dee

Photos

Could you take a photo of us, please?
Può scattarci una foto, per piacere? *(formal)*
pwo skat-tarchee oona foto payr pyachayreh

Where can I develop my photos?
Dove posso sviluppare le mie foto?
doveh posso zveeloop-pareh lay meeeh foto

How much is it to develop them?
Quanto costa far sviluppare?
kwanto kosta far zveeloop-pareh

batteries (lithium ~)	**batterie** (f.) **(al litio)**	bat-tayreeeh (al-leetyo)
digital camera	**una fotocamera digitale**	oona fotokamayra deejeetaleh
disposable camera	**una macchina fotografica usa e getta**	oona mak-keena foto-grafeeka ooza ay jet-ta
SD memory card	**una scheda di memoria SD**	oona skeda dee maymorya esseh-dee

Souvenirs

bracelets	**bracciali** (m.)	brachalee
embroidery	**ricami** (m. pl.)	reekamee
jewellery	**gioielli** (m. pl.)	joyayl-lee
lace	**merletti** (m. pl.) / **pizzi** (m. pl.)	mayrlet-tee / peet-tsee
leather goods	**pelletteria** (f.)	payl-layt-tayreea
necklaces	**collane** (f.)	kol-laneh
pottery	**ceramica** (f.)	chayrameeka
vase	**vaso** (m.)	vazo

↗ Business meetings

If you're in Italy for business, here is some useful vocabulary to help you get by.

Making an appointment

I would like to speak to Mr / Ms ...
Vorrei parlare con il signor... / la signora...
vorrey parlareh kon eel seenyor / la seenyora

Could you set up an appointment for me with Mr / Ms ... ?
Vorrei chiedervi di fissarmi un appuntamento con il signor... / la signora...?
vorrey kyaydayrvee dee feessarmee oon ap-poontamaynto kon eel seenyor / la seenyora

Can I leave a message?
Posso lasciare un messaggio?
posso lashareh oon mayssaj-jo

OK, I'll call back this afternoon / evening / tomorrow morning.
Bene, richiamo nel pomeriggio / stasera / domani mattina.
beneh reekyamo nel pomayreej-jo / stasayra / domanee mat-teena

I'll give you my mobile/cell number …
Le do il mio numero di cellulare...
lay do eel meeo noomayro dee chayl-loolareh

In the workplace

I have a meeting with Mr / Ms …
Ho appuntamento con il signor... / la signora...
o ap-poontamento kon eel seenyor / la seenyora

Could you organize a visit?
Si può organizzare una visita?
see pwo organeed-dsareh oona veezeeta

Can I sit down here to work?
Posso accomodarmi qui per lavorare?
posso ak-komodarmee kwee payr lavorareh

I'd like to send a fax / an email.
Vorrei mandare un fax / un e-mail.
vorrey mandareh oon faks / oon eemayl

Could I use a computer with internet access?
Posso utilizzare un computer con Internet?
posso ooteeleed-dsareh oon kompyooter kon eentayrnayt

Do you have a direct line I can call?
Avete una linea telefonica diretta?
avayteh oona leenaya taylayfoneeka deeret-ta

Business vocabulary

If you need something at **la società** *[sochayta]* the company:

bulletin board	**bacheca** *(f.)*	*bakeka*
cabinets	**armadietti** *(m.)*	*armadyayt-tee*
keyboard	**tastiera** *(f.)*	*tastyayra*
meeting	**riunione** *(f.)*	*reeoonyoneh*
mouse	**mouse** *(m.)*	*maoz*
office	**ufficio** *(m.)*	*oof-feecho*
phone book	**rubrica** *(f.)* **telefonica**	*roobreeka taylayfoneeka*
photocopier	**fotocopiatrice** *(f.)*	*fotokopyatreecheh*
printer	**stampante** *(f.)*	*stampanteh*
rubber stamp	**timbro** *(m.)*	*teembro*
screen	**schermo** *(m.)*	*skayrmo*
screen (projection ~)	**schermo** *(m.)* **di proiezione**	*skayrmo dee proyaytsyoneh*

Conferences and trade shows

I've come for ...	Sono qui per...	*sono kwee payr*
the assembly / meeting.	l'assemblea.	*lassaymblaya*
the board/committee meeting.	la riunione della commissione / del comitato.	*la reeoonyoneh del-la kom-meessyoneh / del komeetato*
the conference.	il congresso.	*eel kongresso*
the exhibition.	la mostra.	*la mostra*
the international conference.	la conferenza internazionale.	*la konfayrentsa eentayrnatsyonaleh*

| the trade show. | la fiera commerciale. | la fyayra kom-mayrchaleh |

Where is the visitor's entrance, please?
Dov'è l'ingresso per i visitatori, per favore?
doveh leengresso payr ee veezeetatoree payr favoreh

I'm looking for the Italian pavilion.
Sto cercando il padiglione italiano.
sto chayrkando eel padeelyoneh eetalyano

Do you have a brochure?
Avete un opuscolo informativo?
avayteh oon opooskolo eenformateevo

Could I have your business card?
Posso avere il suo biglietto da visita?
posso avayreh eel sooo beelyayt-to da veezeeta

↗ Health

If you need medical attention

In case of a health problem (**una problema di salute**):

I'm injured. (m./f.)   *He/she is unwell.*
Sono ferito/-a.   **È malato/-a.**
sono fayreeto/-a   *eh malato/-a*

Quick, call ...	Presto, chiami...	presto kyamee
a doctor!	un medico!	oon medeeko
an ambulance!	un'ambulanza!	oonamboolantsa

CONVERSING

Where can I find a doctor who speaks English?
Dove posso trovare un medico in grado di parlare inglese?
doveh posso trovareh oon medeeko een grado dee parlareh inglayzeh

Where is the hospital?
Dov'è l'ospedale?
doveh lospaydaleh

I'm diabetic. (m./f.)
Sono diabetico/-a.
sono dyabeteeko/-a

I have / He/she has a heart problem.
Soffro / Soffre di mal di cuore.
sof-fro / sof-freh dee mal dee kworeh

I have asthma.
Ho l'asma.
o lazma

Symptoms

Here are some phrases if you need to describe **i suoi sintomi** *your symptoms*:

I have/don't have a fever.
Ho la / Non ho febbre.
o la / non o feb-breh

I feel weak.
Mi sento debole.
mee sento dayboleh

I feel like throwing up. / I have thrown up.
Ho voglia di vomitare. / Ho vomitato.
o volya dee vomeetareh / o vomeetato

I can't move. It hurts.
Non mi posso muovere. Mi fa male.
non mee posso mwovayreh mee fa maleh

I'm dizzy.
Ho le vertigini.
o lay vayrteejeenee

It burns.
Mi brucia.
mee broocha

Health problems

I have / He/she has ...	Ho / Ha...	o / a
chills.	brividi.	breeveedee
convulsions.	convulsioni.	konvoolsyonee
diarrhoea.	diarrea.	dyarraya
dizziness.	stordimento.	stordeemaynto
haemorrhoids.	emorroidi.	aymorroydee
a headache.	mal di testa.	mal dee testa
a sunburn.	scottatura.	skot-tatoora
spasms / cramps.	spasmi / crampi.	spazmee / crampee

arthritis	artrite (f.)	artreeteh
broken	rotto/-a	rot-to/-a
cold	raffreddore (m.)	raf-frayd-doreh
flu	influenza (f.)	eenflooentsa
food poisoning	intossicazione (f.) alimentare	eentosseekatsyoneh aleementareh
hay fever	raffreddore (m.) da fieno	raf-frayd-doreh da fyayno
hernia (or slipped disc)	ernia (f.)	ayrnya
indigestion	indigestione (f.)	eendeejestyoneh
infection	infezione (f.)	eenfaytsyoneh
inflammation	infiammazione (f.)	eenfyam-matsyoneh
microbe / germ	microbo (m.)	meekrobo
pneumonia	polmonite (f.)	polmoneeteh
rheumatism	reumatismo (m.)	rayoomateezmo
sprain / dislocation	slogatura (f.)	zlogatoora
stiff neck	torcicollo (m.)	torcheekol-lo
sunstroke	insolazione (f.)	eensolatsyoneh
torn	strappato/-a	strap-pato/-a
ulcer	ulcera (f.)	oolchayra
virus	virus (m.)	veeroos

CONVERSING

Pains and body parts

To describe the part of your body that hurts, add the relevant word to the phrase below.

My ... hurts / hurt.
Mi fa (sing.) **/ fanno** (pl.) **male...**
mee fa / fan-no maleh

appendix	l'appendice	lap-pendeecheh
bladder	la vescica	la vaysheeka
chest	il torace	eel toracheh
chest (breasts)	il petto	eel pet-to
head	la testa	la testa
heart	il cuore	eel kworeh
hip	l'anca	lanka
joints	le articolazioni	lay arteekolatsyonee
kidney	il rene	eel reneh
liver	il fegato	eel faygato
lungs	il polmone	eel polmoneh
rib	la costola	la kostola
stomach	lo stomaco	lo stomako
tendon	il tendine	eel tendeeneh
throat	la gola	la gola
tonsils	le tonsille	lay tonseel-leh
when I urinate	quando urino	kwando ooreeno

Parts of the body

ankle	la caviglia	la kaveelya
arm	il braccio	eel bracho
back	la schiena	la skyayna

ear	l'orecchio	lorayk-kyo
elbow	il gomito	eel gomeeto
eye / eyes	l'occhio / gli occhi	lok-kyo / lyee ok-kee
face	il volto	eel volto
finger	il dito	eel deeto
foot	il piede	eel pyaydeh
hand	la mano	la mano
knee	il ginocchio	eel jeenok-kyo
leg	la gamba	la gamba
mouth	la bocca	la bok-ka
neck	il collo	eel kol-lo
nose	il naso	eel nazo
shoulder	la spalla	la spal-la
skin	la pelle	la pel-leh
spine	la spina dorsale	la speena dorsaleh
toe	il dito del piede	eel deeto del pyaydeh
wrist	il polso	eel polso

Women's health

contraceptive pill	pillola (f.) anticoncezionale	peel-lola anteekonchaytsyonaleh
gynaecologist	ginecologo/-a	jeenaykologo/-a
maternity clinic	clinica (f.) ostetrica	kleeneeka ostetreeka
menstruation	mestruazioni (f.)	maystrooatsyonee
pads	assorbenti (m.) igienici	assorbentee eejeneechee
pregnancy	gravidanza (f.)	graveedantsa
tampons	assorbenti (m.) interni	assorbentee eentayrnee
ultrasound	ecografia (f.)	aykografeea

I am / She is pregnant.
Sono / È incinta.
*s*o*no / eh eench*ee*nta*

We need to do an ultrasound.
Deve fare un ecografia.
*d*a*yveh fareh* oo*n aykografee*a

Hopefully you won't need these terms, but just in case you do:
la cistite *cystitis* or *urinary tract infection*, **la candidosi** *thrush* or *yeast infection*, **l'emicrania** *migraine*.

Getting treatment

Don't worry, it's nothing serious.
Non si preoccupi, non è niente.
*non see pray*o*koopee non eh n*yay*nteh*

You need to stay in bed for three days.
Deve rimanere a letto per tre giorni.
*d*a*yveh reeman*ay*reh a l*e*t-to payr treh j*o*rnee*

I'm prescribing you an antibiotic.
Le prescrivo un antibiotico.
*lay prayskr*ee*vo oon antee*byo*teeko*

You need to go to the hospital.
Deve andare in ospedale.
*d*a*yveh and*a*reh een ospayd*a*leh*

Some useful words:

bandage	**fasciatura** (f.)	fashat**oo**ra
examination / test	**esame** (m.)	ay**z**ameh
injection / shot	**iniezione** (f.)	eenayts**yo**neh
plaster cast	**gesso** (m.)	**j**esso
X-ray	**radiografia** (f.)	radyograf**ee**a

At the dentist's

Where can I find a dentist who speaks English?
Dove posso trovare un dentista in grado di parlare inglese?
doveh posso trovareh oon daynteesta een grado dee parlareh eenglayzeh

I have an abscess.
Ho un ascesso dentale.
o oon ashesso dayntaleh

This tooth hurts.
Questo dente mi fa male.
kwaysto denteh mee fa maleh

I've lost a filling.
Mi è caduta un'otturazione di piombo.
mee eh kadoota oonot-tooratsyoneh dee pyombo

At the optician's

I've broken my glasses. Can you fix them for me, please?
Ho rotto i miei occhiali. Me li potete riparare per favore?
o rot-to ee meeey ok-kyalee may lee potayteh reepaarareh payr favoreh

I would like some contact lenses.
Vorrei delle lenti a contatto.
vorrey del-leh lentee a kontat-to

At the pharmacy

La farmacia can be spotted by its green cross sign, which is lit up when open. Pharmacists in Italy are highly trained and can often advise on general health issues.

I'm looking for a pharmacy.
Sto cercando una farmacia.
sto chayrkando oona farmacheea

I'd like something for ...	Vorrei qualcosa per...	vorrey kwalkoza payr
a cold.	il raffreddore.	eel raf-frayd-doreh
a cough.	la tosse.	la tosseh
constipation.	la costipazione.	la kosteepatsyoneh
diarrhoea.	la diarrea.	la dyarraya
a headache.	il mal di testa.	eel mal dee testa
seasickness.	il mal di mare.	eel mal dee mareh
sunburns.	le scottature da sole.	lay skot-tatooray da soleh

Note that most health care products can only be found at pharmacies; they aren't sold at supermarkets:

antiseptic cream	crema (f.) antisettica	krema anteeset-teeka
aspirin	aspirina (f.)	aspeereena
contraceptives	contraccettivi (m.)	kontrachayt-teevee
cotton wool	ovatta (f.)	ovat-ta
disinfectant	disinfettante (m.)	deezeenfayt-tanteh
eardrops	gocce (f.) per l'orecchio	gocheh payr lorayk-kyo
eye drops	collirio (m.)	kol-leeryo
gargling solution	gargarismo (m.)	gargareezmo
gauze bandage	benda (f.) di garza	benda dee gartsa
iodine	iodio (m.)	eeodyo
laxative	lassativo (m.)	lassateevo
mouthwash	colluttorio (m.)	kol-loot-toryo
painkiller (or sedative)	calmante (f.)	kalmanteh
plaster / bandaid	cerotto (m.) adesivo	chayrot-to adayzeevo
sleeping pills	sonniferi (m.)	son-neefayree
thermometer	termometro (m.)	tayrmomaytro
throat lozenges	pastiglie (f.) per la gola	pasteelyeh payr la gola

Assimil is on Facebook:

www.facebook.com/editions.assimil

- → latest news
- → exclusive content
- → competitions
- → Assimil's history
- → latest releases
- → audio samples and more

Join us on our other networks:

vimeo.com/assimil

soundcloud.com/assimil

twitter.com/EditionsAssimil

www.youtube.com/user/MethodeASSIMIL

Subscribe to Assimil's newsletter:
www.assimil.com

Index

A
A/an (article) **29–30**
Abbreviations **80–81**
Accepting invitations **70–71**
Accidents **78–79, 147–148**
Accommodation **111–115**
Activities **94–95, 100–101, 102–105**
Addresses **63, 87**
Addressing someone **19–20, 47–48, 57**
Adjectives **15, 18**
Age **51, 63–64**
Agreeing and disagreeing **59**
Ailments **147–152**
Air travel **82–83**
Animals **108–110**
Apologizing **49**
Appointments **144–145**
Assistance **78–79, 147**

B
Banks **99–100**
Bathroom **80**
Be (verb) **16, 20, 26, 32, 39, 45, 53, 55**
Beaches **104–105**
Beverages **31, 39, 41, 136–137, 139**
Biking **88**
Bill (check) **119**
Boat travel **86–87**
Body parts **150–151**
Booking **87, 111–112, 116–117**
Books **139, 140**
Breakdown (car) **89–90**
Breakfast **29, 112–113**
Bus travel **83–85, 92–93**
Business **144–147**

C
Camping **105–107**
Can (verb) **49–50**
Car travel **88–92**
Celebrations **58–59, 77–78**
Changing money **82**
Chatting up **71–73**
Checking out **113**
Cheese **134–135**
Chemist's **153–154**
Clothes **141–143**
Coach travel **83–85**
Coffee **41, 113, 137**
Colours **141**
Complaints (hotel / restaurant) **115, 120**
Computers **97–98, 114, 145**
Conditional **41–42**
Conferences **146–147**
Cooking **130–131**
Crime **99**
Cuisine **120–125, 132–135**
Customs **81**
Cycling **88**

D
Dates (calendar) **75–76**
Dating **71–73**
Days of the week **76**

Definite article **18, 22, 23, 24, 42**
Dentist **153**
Directions **92**
Disagreeing **59**
Do (verb) **48**
Doctor **147–148, 152**
Drinks **31, 39, 41, 136–137, 139**
Driving **88–92**
Dry cleaner **114, 140–141**

E
Eating **37–38, 116–135**
Emergencies **78–79, 147**
Employment **65–67**
Excusing oneself **60, 61, 71**
Eyes **151, 153**

F
Family **64–65**
Feelings **69–70**
Feminine/masculine **15–16, 18**
Films **49, 53–54, 100–101**
Finding your way **92**
Fish **110, 122, 127–128, 131, 139**
Flying **82–83**
Food **116–135**
Formal/informal address **19–20, 47–48, 55–56, 57, 61**
Fruit **130**
Future tense **36, 43, 55**

G
Gender (grammatical) **15–16, 18**
Gerund **31–32**
Gifts **144**
Glasses **153**

Go (verb) **26**
Going out **27–28, 70–71, 100–101**
Greetings **57**

H
Hairdresser **101–102, 139**
Have (verb) **20, 34, 37, 38**
Have to (verb) **38, 49–50**
Health **147–154**
Help **78–79, 147**
Hiking **103–104, 106–107**
Holidays **58–59, 77–78**
Hospital **148, 152**
Hotels **111–115**

I
Illnesses **147–152**
Imperative (commands) **38, 44, 46, 48, 53–54, 55–56**
Indefinite article **29–30**
Informal/formal address **19–20, 47–48, 55–56, 57, 61**
Injuries **147–148**
Internet **97–98, 114, 145**
Introductions **21–22, 62**
Invitations **49–50, 70–71**

J
Jobs **65–67**

L
Languages **60**
Laundry **114, 140–141**
Like (verb) **27–28, 42, 69**
Lodging **111–115**
Lost property **99**

INDEX

Love **71–73**
Luggage **82**

M

Maps **140**
Marital status **64**
Markets **95, 139**
Masculine/feminine **15–16, 18**
Meals **116**
Meat **121–122, 126–127, 131, 139**
Medical issues **147–152**
Meeting people **21–22, 61–73**
Meetings (business) **145–146**
Messages (telephone) **145**
Money **82, 99–100**
Months of the year **76**
More/less **36**
Mr/Mrs/Miss **57**
Museums **94–95**
Music **27, 100–101**
Must/should **38, 49–50**

N

Names **51–52, 62**
Nationalities **62–63**
Negative form **18, 53–54, 56**
Newspapers **139, 140**
Numbers *cover flap*

O

Occupations **65–67**
Online **97–98, 114, 145**
Opinions **69–70**
Optician **153**
Ordering (restaurant) **31, 39, 41**
Outdoor activities **102–107**

P

Pains **150–151**
Parking **91, 114**
Passport **81**
Past participle **34, 45–46, 52**
Past tense **34, 35–36, 38, 39, 52, 53**
Paying **88, 113, 119–120, 138**
Performances **100–101**
Pharmacy **153–154**
Phoning **19–20, 31, 49, 96–97, 144–146**
Photos **95, 143–144**
Places of interest **94–95**
Plants **108**
Please **32, 59**
Plural forms **15–16, 18, 25, 30**
Police **78–79, 99, 139**
Politeness **54, 55, 57**
Possession **22, 33, 34**
Post office **95–96, 139**
Present tense **22, 24, 26, 32, 36, 40, 48, 50**
Problems **78–79, 81, 89–90, 99, 115, 143**
Professions **65–67**
Pronouns **17, 20, 26, 28, 44, 52, 53**
Public holidays **77–78**

Q

Questions **16, 20, 59**

R

Rail travel **35–36, 55–56, 83–86**
Recreation **102–107**
Reflexive verbs **51–52**
Religion **67–68**